D0596864

Dare To Succeed

A Treasury of
Inspiration and Wisdom
for Life and Career

Dare To Succeed

A Treasury of
Inspiration and Wisdom
for Life and Career

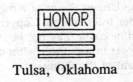

Tulsa, Oklahoma

Unless otherwise indicated, all Scripture quotations are taken from the *King James Version* of the Bible.

Dare To Succeed —
A Treasury of Inspiration and Wisdom
for Life and Career
ISBN 1-56292-001-4
Copyright © 1991 by Honor Books
P. O. Box 55388
Tulsa, Oklahoma 74155

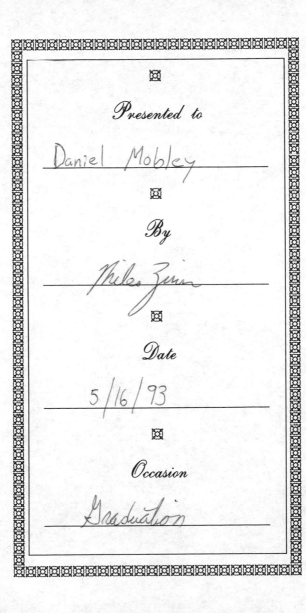

Presented to

Daniel Mobley

By

Miles Zinn

Date

5/16/93

Occasion

Graduation

CONTENTS

Part III — Motivation and Guidance

Part IV — Quotes From Great Leaders

Part V — 31-Day Devotional
by John Mason

Introduction

This book was created especially for you. It is specifically designed to provide you with the means to gain wisdom, motivation and inspiration, to set goals and to achieve them — and for what purpose? To help you daily in your career and throughout your life!

In the last few years, life has become increasingly hurried and confused. Rapidly changing technology, a fluctuating economy, political upheaval around the world, wars and threats of wars have caused many people to have difficulty just making sense of life, much less succeeding in it. But God wants each of us to succeed — in our careers, our lives, our daily walk with Him. For this reason, we have published *Dare To Succeed*; we want the power of the Scriptures, the earnestness of special prayers, the wisdom of renowned leaders and the teachings of learned scholars and teachers to be a blessing to you — one that will help you find success in your career and life.

The book is divided into six parts. Each part contains a different kind of information to help and inspire you to dare to succeed. Here is a brief description and guide to using each part.

Part 1 contains a special collection of Scriptures. These deal primarily with two different areas in your life — successful relationships with God and with others, and with having your needs met.

Part 2 contains powerful prayers for your life. Salvation, commitment, career and relationships are all covered.

Part 3 is a collection of motivational teachings from noted authors Og Mandino, Van Crouch and R. Henry Migliore. Each gives his own distinct perspective on just what it takes to succeed.

Part 4 contains both informational and inspirational remarks about life and living from leaders in a variety of fields — Winston Churchill to John Wooden, Will Rogers to J.C. Penney.

Part 5 is a 31-day devotional by John Mason. This will give you daily encouragement and show you how to find the success in life that you need.

A well thought-out plan for reading the entire Bible is provided in Part 6. As you read through the Bible, day by day, you will find yourself strengthened and encouraged.

Do as God wants you to do — *Dare To Succeed*.

Part I
Wisdom through
the Scriptures

1
Developing your
relationship with God

Jesus, Your Savior

And as Moses lifted up the serpent in the wilderness, even so must the Son of man be lifted up:

That whosoever believeth in him should not perish, but have eternal life.

For God so loved the world, that he gave his only begotten Son, that whosoever believeth in him should not perish, but have everlasting life.

For God sent not his Son into the world to condemn the world; but that the world through him might be saved.

He that believeth on him is not condemned: but he that believeth not is condemned already, because he hath not believed in the name of the only begotten Son of God.

John 3:14-18

And this is the will of him that sent me, that every one which seeth the Son, and believeth on him, may have everlasting life: and I will raise him up at the last day.

John 6:40

Jesus answered and said unto him, Verily, verily, I say unto thee, Except a man be born again, he cannot see the kingdom of God.

John 3:3

Verily, verily, I say unto you, He that believeth on me hath everlasting life.

I am that bread of life.

John 6:47,48

For as the Father raiseth up the dead, and quickeneth them; even so the Son quickeneth whom he will.

For the Father judgeth no man, but hath committed all judgment unto the Son:

That all men should honour the Son, even as they honour the Father. He that honoureth not the Son honoureth not the Father which hath sent him.

Verily, verily, I say unto you, He that heareth my word, and believeth on him that sent me, hath everlasting life, and shall not come into condemnation; but is passed from death unto life.

Verily, verily, I say unto you, The hour is coming, and now is, when the dead shall hear the voice of the Son of God: and they that hear shall live.

For as the Father hath life in himself; so hath he given to the Son to have life in himself.

John 5:21-26

And he said unto them, Ye are from beneath; I am from above: ye are of this world; I am not of this world.

I said therefore unto you, that ye shall die in your sins: for if ye believe not that I am he, ye shall die in your sins.

John 8:23,24

The Father loveth the Son, and hath given all things into his hand.

He that believeth on the Son hath everlasting life: and he that believeth not the Son shall not see life; but the wrath of God abideth on him.

John 3:35,36

The thief cometh not, but for to steal, and to kill, and to destroy: I am come that they might have life, and that they might have it more abundantly.

John 10:10

For there is one God, and one mediator between God and men, the man Christ Jesus;

19

Who gave himself a ransom for all, to be testified in due time.

1 Timothy 2:5,6

Jesus cried and said, He that believeth on me, believeth not on me, but on him that sent me.

And he that seeth me seeth him that sent me.

I am come a light into the world, that whosoever believeth on me should not abide in darkness.

John 12:44-46

My sheep hear my voice, and I know them, and they follow me:

And I give unto them eternal life; and they shall never perish, neither shall any man pluck them out of my hand.

My Father, which gave them me, is greater than all; and no man is able to pluck them out of my Father's hand.

I and my Father are one.

John 10:27-30

Jesus said unto her, I am the resurrection, and the life: he that believeth in me, though he were dead, yet shall he live:

And whosoever liveth and believeth in me shall never die. Believest thou this?

John 11:25,26

Jesus saith unto him, I am the way, the truth, and the life: no man cometh unto the Father, but by me.

John 14:6

And it shall come to pass, that whosoever shall call on the name of the Lord shall be saved.

Acts 2:21

Then Peter said unto them, Repent, and be baptized every one of you in the name of Jesus Christ for the remission of sins, and ye shall receive the gift of the Holy Ghost.

Acts 2:38

Repent ye therefore, and be converted, that your sins may be blotted out, when the times of refreshing shall come from the presence of the Lord.

Acts 3:19

Be it known unto you all, and to all the people of Israel, that by the name of Jesus Christ of Nazareth, whom ye crucified, whom God raised from the dead, even by him doth this man stand here before you whole.

This is the stone which was set at nought of you builders, which is become the head of the corner.

Neither is there salvation in any other: for there is none other name under heaven given among men, whereby we must be saved.

Acts 4:10-12

But we believe that through the grace of the Lord Jesus Christ we shall be saved, even as they.

Acts 15:11

For by grace are ye saved through faith; and that not of yourselves: it is the gift of God:

Not of works, lest any man should boast.

Ephesians 2:8,9

That if thou shalt confess with thy mouth the Lord Jesus, and shalt believe in thine heart that God hath raised him from the dead, thou shalt be saved.

For with the heart man believeth unto righteousness; and with the mouth confession is made unto salvation.

Romans 10:9,10

For Christ also hath once suffered for sins, the just for the unjust, that he might bring us to God, being put to death in the flesh, but quickened by the Spirit.

1 Peter 3:18

But as many as received him, to them gave he power to become the sons of God, even to them that believe on his name:

Which were born, not of blood, nor of the will
of the flesh, nor of the will of man, but of God.
John 1:12,13

Examples of God's Character in the Bible

The LORD is my strength and my shield; my
heart trusted in him, and I am helped: therefore
my heart greatly rejoiceth; and with my song will
I praise him.
Psalm 28:7

O taste and see that the LORD is good:
blessed is the man that trusteth in him.
Psalm 34:8

Who is like unto thee, O LORD, among the
gods? who is like thee, glorious in holiness,
fearful in praises, doing wonders?

Thou stretchedst out thy right hand, the earth
swallowed them.

Thou in thy mercy hast led forth the people
which thou hast redeemed: thou hast guided
them in thy strength unto thy holy habitation.
Exodus 15:11-13

The LORD is my light and my salvation;
whom shall I fear? the LORD is the strength of
my life; of whom shall I be afraid?
Psalm 27:1

The LORD is my strength and song, and he is become my salvation: he is my God, and I will prepare him an habitation; my father's God, and I will exalt him.

The LORD is a man of war: the LORD is his name.

Exodus 15:2,3

And the LORD descended in the cloud, and stood with him there, and proclaimed the name of the LORD.

And the LORD passed by before him, and proclaimed, The LORD, The LORD God, merciful and gracious, longsuffering, and abundant in goodness and truth,

Keeping mercy for thousands, forgiving iniquity and transgression and sin, and that will by no means clear the guilty; visiting the iniquity of the fathers upon the children, and upon the children's children, unto the third and to the fourth generation.

Exodus 34:5-7

The LORD also will be a refuge for the oppressed, a refuge in times of trouble.

And they that know thy name will put their trust in thee: for thou, LORD, hast not forsaken them that seek thee.

Psalm 9:9,10

I will love thee, O LORD, my strength.

The LORD is my rock, and my fortress, and my deliverer; my God, my strength, in whom I will trust; my buckler, and the horn of my salvation, and my high tower.

I will call upon the LORD, who is worthy to be praised: so shall I be saved from mine enemies.

Psalm 18:1-3

Oh how great is thy goodness, which thou hast laid up for them that fear thee; which thou hast wrought for them that trust in thee before the sons of men!

Thou shalt hide them in the secret of thy presence from the pride of man: thou shalt keep them secretly in a pavilion from the strife of tongues.

Psalm 31:19,20

Thou art my hiding place; thou shalt preserve me from trouble; thou shalt compass me about with songs of deliverance. Selah.

Psalm 32:7

Behold, the eye of the LORD is upon them that fear him, upon them that hope in his mercy;

To deliver their soul from death, and to keep them alive in famine.

Our soul waiteth for the LORD: he is our help and our shield.

For our heart shall rejoice in him, because we have trusted in his holy name.

Let thy mercy, O LORD, be upon us, according as we hope in thee.

Psalm 33:18-22

And one cried unto another, and said, Holy, holy, holy, is the LORD of hosts: the whole earth is full of his glory.

Isaiah 6:3

Let your conversation be without covetousness; and be content with such things as ye have: for he hath said, I will never leave thee, nor forsake thee.

So that we may boldly say, The Lord is my helper, and I will not fear what man shall do unto me.

Hebrews 13:5,6

God is faithful, by whom ye were called unto the fellowship of his Son Jesus Christ our Lord.

1 Corinthians 1:9

The righteous cry, and the LORD heareth, and delivereth them out of all their troubles.

The LORD is nigh unto them that are of a broken heart; and saveth such as be of a contrite spirit.

Psalm 34:17,18

But the salvation of the righteous is of the LORD: he is their strength in the time of trouble.

And the LORD shall help them, and deliver them: he shall deliver them from the wicked, and save them, because they trust in him.

Psalm 37:39,40

Blessed is the man whom thou choosest, and causest to approach unto thee, that he may dwell in thy courts: we shall be satisfied with the goodness of thy house, even of thy holy temple.

Psalm 65:4

Like as a father pitieth his children, so the LORD pitieth them that fear him.

For he knoweth our frame; he remembereth that we are dust.

Psalm 103:13,14

For the LORD God is a sun and shield: the LORD will give grace and glory: no good thing will he withhold from them that walk uprightly.

O LORD of hosts, blessed is the man that trusteth in thee.

Psalm 84:11,12

He that dwelleth in the secret place of the most High shall abide under the shadow of the Almighty.

I will say of the LORD, He is my refuge and my fortress: my God; in him will I trust.

Surely he shall deliver thee from the snare of the fowler, and from the noisome pestilence.

He shall cover thee with his feathers, and under his wings shalt thou trust: his truth shall be thy shield and buckler.

Psalm 91:1-4

The works of the LORD are great, sought out of all them that have pleasure therein.

His work is honourable and glorious: and his righteousness endureth for ever.

He hath made his wonderful works to be remembered: the LORD is gracious and full of compassion.

He hath given meat unto them that fear him: he will ever be mindful of his covenant.

He hath shewed his people the power of his works, that he may give them the heritage of the heathen.

The works of his hands are verity and judgment; all his commandments are sure.

They stand fast for ever and ever, and are done in truth and uprightness.

He sent redemption unto his people: he hath commanded his covenant for ever: holy and reverend is his name.

Psalm 111:2-9

That which we have seen and heard declare we unto you, that ye also may have fellowship with us: and truly our fellowship is with the Father, and with his Son Jesus Christ.

And these things write we unto you, that your joy may be full.

1 John 1:3,4

But if we walk in the light, as he is in the light, we have fellowship one with another, and the blood of Jesus Christ his Son cleanseth us from all sin.

1 John 1:7

The LORD is on my side; I will not fear: what can man do unto me?

Psalm 118:6

But Zion said, The LORD hath forsaken me, and my Lord hath forgotten me.

Can a woman forget her sucking child, that she should not have compassion on the son of her womb? yea, they may forget, yet will I not forget thee.

Behold, I have graven thee upon the palms of my hands; thy walls are continually before me.

Isaiah 49:14-16

For thus saith the high and lofty One that inhabiteth eternity, whose name is Holy; I dwell in the high and holy place, with him also that is of a contrite and humble spirit, to revive the spirit of the humble, and to revive the heart of the contrite ones.

Isaiah 57:15

What? know ye not that he which is joined to an harlot is one body? for two, saith he, shall be one flesh.

But he that is joined unto the Lord is one spirit.

Flee fornication. Every sin that a man doeth is without the body; but he that committeth fornication sinneth against his own body.

1 Corinthians 6:16-18

For this is the covenant that I will make with the house of Israel after those days, saith the Lord; I will put my laws into their mind, and write them in their hearts: and I will be to them a God, and they shall be to me a people:

And they shall not teach every man his neighbour, and every man his brother, saying, Know the Lord: for all shall know me, from the least to the greatest.

Hebrews 8:10,11

And the scripture was fulfilled which saith, Abraham believed God, and it was imputed unto him for righteousness: and he was called the Friend of God.

James 2:23

And I will walk among you, and will be your God, and ye shall be my people.

Leviticus 26:12

The Lord is not slack concerning his promise, as some men count slackness; but is longsuffering to us-ward, not willing that any should perish, but that all should come to repentance.

2 Peter 3:9

Who will have all men to be saved, and to come unto the knowledge of the truth.

1 Timothy 2:4

Sharing With God in Prayer

And this is the confidence that we have in him, that, if we ask any thing according to his will, he heareth us:

And if we know that he hear us, whatsoever we ask, we know that we have the petitions that we desired of him.

1 John 5:14,15

Come and hear, all ye that fear God, and I will declare what he hath done for my soul.

I cried unto him with my mouth, and he was extolled with my tongue.

If I regard iniquity in my heart, the Lord will not hear me:

But verily God hath heard me; he hath attended to the voice of my prayer.

Blessed be God, which hath not turned away my prayer, nor his mercy from me.

Psalm 66:16-20

I, even I, am he that blotteth out thy transgressions for mine own sake, and will not remember thy sins.

Put me in remembrance: let us plead together: declare thou, that thou mayest be justified.

Isaiah 43:25-26

That which we have seen and heard declare we unto you, that ye also may have fellowship with us: and truly our fellowship is with the Father, and with his Son Jesus Christ.

1 John 1:3

I sought the LORD, and he heard me, and delivered me from all my fears.

They looked unto him, and were lightened: and their faces were not ashamed.

This poor man cried, and the LORD heard him, and saved him out of all his troubles.

The angel of the LORD encampeth round about them that fear him, and delivereth them.

Psalm 34:4-7

Seeking God's Face With Your Whole Heart

Trust in him at all times; ye people, pour out your heart before him: God is a refuge for us. Selah.

Psalm 62:8

One thing have I desired of the LORD, that will I seek after; that I may dwell in the house of the LORD all the days of my life, to behold the beauty of the LORD, and to inquire in his temple.

Psalm 27:4

When thou saidst, Seek ye my face; my heart said unto thee, Thy face, LORD, will I seek.

Hide not thy face far from me; put not thy servant away in anger: thou hast been my help;

leave me not, neither forsake me, O God of my salvation.

Psalm 27:8,9

O fear the LORD, ye his saints: for there is no want to them that fear him.

The young lions do lack, and suffer hunger: but they that seek the LORD shall not want any good thing.

Psalm 34:9-10

As the hart panteth after the water brooks, so panteth my soul after thee, O God.

My soul thirsteth for God, for the living God: when shall I come and appear before God?

Psalm 42:1,2

O God, thou art my God; early will I seek thee: my soul thirsteth for thee, my flesh longeth for thee in a dry and thirsty land, where no water is;

To see thy power and thy glory, so [as] I have seen thee in the sanctuary.

Because thy lovingkindness is better than life, my lips shall praise thee.

Thus will I bless thee while I live: I will lift up my hands in thy name.

Psalm 63:1-4

The humble shall see this, and be glad: and your heart shall live that seek God.

Psalm 69:32

Nevertheless I am continually with thee: thou hast holden me by my right hand.

Thou shalt guide me with thy counsel, and afterward receive me to glory.

Whom have I in heaven but thee? and there is none upon earth that I desire beside thee.

My flesh and my heart faileth: but God is the strength of my heart, and my portion for ever.

For, lo, they that are far from thee shall perish: thou hast destroyed all them that go a whoring from thee.

But it is good for me to draw near to God: I have put my trust in the Lord GOD, that I may declare all thy works.

Psalm 73:23-28

My soul longeth, yea, even fainteth for the courts of the LORD: my heart and my flesh crieth out for the living God.

Psalm 84:2

The LORD looked down from heaven upon the children of men, to see if there were any that did understand, and seek God.

Psalm 14:2

This is the generation of them that seek him, that seek thy face, O Jacob. Selah.

Psalm 24:6

Glory ye in his holy name: let the heart of them rejoice that seek the LORD.

Seek the LORD, and his strength: seek his face evermore.

Psalm 105:3,4

Yea, in the way of thy judgments, O LORD, have we waited for thee; the desire of our soul is to thy name, and to the remembrance of thee.

With my soul have I desired thee in the night; yea, with my spirit within me will I seek thee early: for when thy judgments are in the earth, the inhabitants of the world will learn righteousness.

Isaiah 26:8,9

But what things were gain to me, those I counted loss for Christ.

Yea doubtless, and I count all things but loss for the excellency of the knowledge of Christ Jesus my Lord: for whom I have suffered the loss of all things, and do count them but dung, that I may win Christ.

And be found in him, not having mine own righteousness, which is of the law, but that which is through the faith of Christ, the righteousness which is of God by faith:

That I may know him, and the power of his resurrection, and the fellowship of his sufferings, being made conformable unto his death;

If by any means I might attain unto the resurrection of the dead.

Not as though I had already attained, either were already perfect: but I follow after, if that I may apprehend that for which also I am apprehended of Christ Jesus.

Philippians 3:7-12

Draw nigh to God, and he will draw nigh to you. Cleanse your hands, ye sinners; and purify your hearts, ye doubled minded.

James 4:8

With my whole heart have I sought thee: O let me not wander from thy commandments.

Psalm 119:10

And thou shalt love the LORD thy God with all thine heart, and with all thy soul, and with all thy might.

Deuteronomy 6:5

Take good heed therefore unto yourselves, that ye love the LORD your God.

Joshua 23:11

Loving God Through Praise and Worship

Rejoice in the Lord alway: and again I say, Rejoice.

Philippians 4:4

Whoso offereth praise glorifieth me: and to him that ordereth his conversation aright will I shew the salvation of God.

Psalm 50:23

Be thou exalted, LORD, in thine own strength: so will we sing and praise thy power.

Psalm 21:13

Rejoice in the LORD, O ye righteous: for praise is comely for the upright.

Praise the LORD with harp: sing unto him with the psaltery and an instrument of ten strings.

Sing unto him a new song; play skilfully with a loud noise.

Psalm 33:1-3

Oh that men would praise the LORD for his goodness, and for his wonderful works to the children of men!

For he satisfieth the longing soul, and filleth the hungry soul with goodness.

Psalm 107:8,9

Offer the sacrifices of righteousness, and put your trust in the LORD.

Psalm 4:5

I will praise thee, O LORD, with my whole heart; I will shew forth all thy marvellous works.

I will be glad and rejoice in thee: I will sing praise to thy name, O thou most High.

Psalm 9:1,2

O love the LORD, all ye his saints: for the LORD preserveth the faithful, and plentifully rewardeth the proud doer.

Be of good courage, and he shall strengthen your heart, all ye that hope in the LORD.

Psalm 31:23,24

I will bless the LORD at all times: his praise shall continually be in my mouth.

My soul shall make her boast in the LORD: the humble shall hear thereof, and be glad.

O magnify the LORD with me, and let us exalt his name together.

Psalm 34:1-3

O come, let us sing unto the LORD: let us make a joyful noise to the rock of our salvation.

Let us come before his presence with thanksgiving, and make a joyful noise unto him with psalms.

For the LORD is a great God, and a great King above all gods.

Psalms 95:1-3

If ye love me, keep my commandments.

John 14:15

Sing and rejoice, O daughter of Zion: for, lo, I come, and I will dwell in the midst of thee, saith the LORD.

Zechariah 2:10

2

YOUR RELATIONSHIPS

Conflict at Home in Your Family

Blessed are the peacemakers: for they shall be called the children of God.

Matthew 5:9

Judge not, and ye shall not be judged: condemn not, and ye shall not be condemned: forgive, and ye shall be forgiven.

Luke 6:37

Wherefore, my beloved brethren, let every man be swift to hear, slow to speak, slow to wrath:

For the wrath of man worketh not the righteousness of God.

James 1:19-20

Be ye angry, and sin not: let not the sun go down upon your wrath:

Neither give place to the devil.

41

Let him that stole steal no more: but rather let him labour, working with his hands the thing which is good, that he may have to give to him that needeth.

Let no corrupt communication proceed out of your mouth, but that which is good to the use of edifying, that it may minister grace unto the hearers.

And grieve not the holy Spirit of God, whereby ye are sealed unto the day of redemption.

Let all bitterness, and wrath, and anger, and clamour, and evil speaking, be put away from you, with all malice:

And be ye kind one to another, tender-hearted, forgiving one another, even as God for Christ's sake hath forgiven you.

Ephesians 4:26-32

But if ye have bitter envying and strife in your hearts, glory not, and lie not against the truth.

This wisdom descendeth not from above, but is earthly, sensual, devilish.

For where envying and strife is, there is confusion and every evil work.

But the wisdom that is from above is first pure, then peaceable, gentle, and easy to be intreated, full of mercy and good fruits, without partiality, and without hypocrisy.

And the fruit of righteousness is sown in peace of them that make peace.

James 3:14-18

A soft answer turneth away wrath: but grievous words stir up anger.

The tongue of the wise useth knowledge aright: but the mouth of fools poureth out foolishness.

The eyes of the LORD are in every place, beholding the evil and the good.

A wholesome tongue is a tree of life: but perverseness therein is a breach in the spirit.

Proverbs 15:1-4

Put on therefore, as the elect of God, holy and beloved, bowels of mercies, kindness, humbleness of mind, meekness, longsuffering;

Forbearing one another, and forgiving one another, if any man have a quarrel against any: even as Christ forgave you, so also do ye.

And above all these things put on charity, which is the bond of perfectness.

Colossians 3:12-14

Hatred stirreth up strifes: but love covereth all sins.

Proverbs 10:12

Finding Godly Friends

He that walketh with wise men shall be wise: but a companion of fools shall be destroyed.

Proverbs 13:20

A friend loveth at all times, and a brother is born for adversity.

Proverbs 17:17

Can two walk together, except they be agreed?

Amos 3:3

Ye adulterers and adulteresses, know ye not that the friendship of the world is enmity with God? whosoever therefore will be a friend of the world is the enemy of God.

James 4:4

Whoso keepeth the law is a wise son: but he that is a companion of riotous men shameth his father.

Proverbs 28:7

Go from the presence of a foolish man, when thou perceivest not in him the lips of knowledge.

Proverbs 14:7

Make no friendship with an angry man; and with a furious man thou shalt not go:

Lest thou learn his ways, and get a snare to thy soul.

Proverbs 22:24,25

Thy princes are rebellious, and companions of thieves: every one loveth gifts, and followeth after rewards: they judge not the fatherless, neither doth the cause of the widow come unto them.

Isaiah 1:23

Partly, whilst ye were made a gazingstock both by reproaches and afflictions; and partly, whilst ye became companions of them that were so used.

Hebrews 10:33

A man that hath friends must shew himself friendly: and there is a friend that sticketh closer than a brother.

Proverbs 18:24

Ointment and perfume rejoice the heart: so doth the sweetness of a man's friend by hearty counsel.

Proverbs 27:9

Flee also youthful lusts: but follow righteousness, faith, charity, peace, with them that call on the Lord out of a pure heart.

2 Timothy 2:22

Blessed is the man that walketh not in the counsel of the ungodly, nor standeth in the way of sinners, nor sitteth in the seat of the scornful.

But his delight is in the law of the LORD; and in his law doth he meditate day and night.

And he shall be like a tree planted by the rivers of water, that bringeth forth his fruit in his season; his leaf also shall not wither; and whatsoever he doeth shall prosper.

Psalm 1:1-3

I am a companion of all them that fear thee, and of them that keep thy precepts.

Psalm 119:63

That thou mayest walk in the way of good men, and keep the paths of the righteous.

Proverbs 2:20

We took sweet counsel together, and walked unto the house of God in company.

Psalm 55:14

Finding the Right Kind of Person To Date

Be ye not unequally yoked together with unbelievers: for what fellowship hath righteousness with unrighteousness? and what communion hath light with darkness?

And what concord hath Christ with Belial? or what part hath he that believeth with an infidel?

And what agreement hath the temple of God with idols? for ye are the temple of the living God; as God hath said, I will dwell in them, and walk in them; and I will be their God, and they shall be my people.

Wherefore come out from among them, and be ye separate, saith the Lord, and touch not the unclean thing; and I will receive you,

And will be a Father unto you, and ye shall be my sons and daughters, saith the Lord Almighty.

2 Corinthians 6:14-18

Flee also youthful lusts: but follow righteousness, faith, charity, peace, with them that call on the Lord out of a pure heart.

2 Timothy 2:22

Make no friendship with an angry man; and with a furious man thou shalt not go.

Proverbs 22:24

Now the God of patience and consolation grant you to be likeminded one toward another according to Christ Jesus:

That ye may with one mind and one mouth glorify God, even the Father of our Lord Jesus Christ.

Romans 15:5,6

But let it be the hidden man of the heart, in that which is not corruptible, even the ornament of a meek and quiet spirit, which is in the sight of God of great price.

1 Peter 3:4

If there be therefore any consolation in Christ, if any comfort of love, if any fellowship of the Spirit, if any bowels and mercies,

Fulfil ye my joy, that ye be likeminded, having the same love, being of one accord, of one mind.

Let nothing be done through strife or vainglory; but in lowliness of mind let each esteem other better than themselves.

Look not every man on his own things, but every man also on the things of others.

Philippians 2:1-4

Having therefore these promises, dearly beloved, let us cleanse ourselves from all filthiness of the flesh and spirit, perfecting holiness in the fear of God.

2 Corinthians 7:1

I wrote unto you in an epistle not to company with fornicators.

1 Corinthians 5:9

But now I have written unto you not to keep company, if any man that is called a brother be a fornicator, or covetous, or an idolater, or a railer, or a drunkard, or an extortioner; with such an one no not to eat.

1 Corinthians 5:11

I am a companion of all them that fear thee, and of them that keep thy precepts.

Psalm 119:63

Let no corrupt communication proceed out of your mouth, but that which is good to the use of edifying, that it may minister grace unto the hearers.

Ephesians 4:29

Let your speech be alway with grace, seasoned with salt, that ye may know how ye ought to answer every man.

Colossians 4:6

She openeth her mouth with wisdom; and in her tongue is the law of kindness.

Proverbs 31:26

Who can find a virtuous woman? for her price is far above rubies.

Proverbs 31:10

And to knowledge temperance; and to temperance patience; and to patience godliness;

And to godliness brotherly kindness; and to brotherly kindness charity.

2 Peter 1:6,7

For he that will love life, and see good days, let him refrain his tongue from evil, and his lips that they speak no guile:

Let him eschew evil, and do good; let him seek peace, and ensue it.

1 Peter 3:10,11

And he spake unto the congregation, saying, Depart, I pray you, from the tents of these wicked men, and touch nothing of theirs, lest ye be consumed in all their sins.

Numbers 16:26

A froward heart shall depart from me: I will not know a wicked person.

Psalm 101:4

He that worketh deceit shall not dwell within my house: he that telleth lies shall not tarry in my sight.

Psalm 101:7

He that goeth about as a talebearer revealeth secrets: therefore meddle not with him that flattereth with his lips.

Proverbs 20:19

Now we command you, brethren, in the name of our Lord Jesus Christ, that ye withdraw yourselves from every brother that walketh disorderly, and not after the tradition which he received of us.

2 Thessalonians 3:6

Trusting God for a Mate

Delight thyself also in the LORD; and he shall give thee the desires of thine heart.

Psalm 37:4

And the LORD God said, It is not good that the man should be alone; I will make him an help meet for him.

Genesis 2:18

Be not ye therefore like unto them: for your Father knoweth what things ye have need of, before ye ask him.

Matthew 6:8

That ye be not slothful, but followers of them who through faith and patience inherit the promises.

Hebrews 6:12

Whoso findeth a wife findeth a good thing, and obtaineth favour of the LORD.

Proverbs 18:22

And the LORD shall guide thee continually, and satisfy thy soul in drought, and make fat thy bones: and thou shalt be like a watered garden, and like a spring of water, whose waters fail not.
Isaiah 58:11

House and riches are the inheritance of fathers: and a prudent wife is from the LORD.
Proverbs 19:14

The LORD is nigh unto all them that call upon him, to all that call upon him in truth.

He will fulfil the desire of them that fear him: he also will hear their cry, and will save them.
Psalm 145:18,19

But let patience have her perfect work, that ye may be perfect and entire, wanting nothing.
James 1:4

Thou shalt no more be termed Forsaken; neither shall thy land any more be termed Desolate: but thou shalt be called Hephzibah, and thy land Beulah: for the LORD delighteth in thee, and thy land shall be married.

For as a young man marrieth a virgin, so shall thy sons marry thee: and as the bridegroom rejoiceth over the bride, so shall thy God rejoice over thee.

Isaiah 62:4,5

For the LORD God is a sun and shield: the LORD will give grace and glory: no good thing will he withhold from them that walk uprightly.

Psalm 84:11

Grant thee according to thine own heart, and fulfil all thy counsel.

Psalm 20:4

3
BIBLE PROMISES
IN TIMES OF NEED

Bible Promises for Gaining Ability

I can do all things through Christ which strengtheneth me.

Philippians 4:13

I thank my God always on your behalf, for the grace of God which is given you by Jesus Christ;

That in every thing ye are enriched by him, in all utterance, and in all knowledge;

Even as the testimony of Christ was confirmed in you:

So that ye come behind in no gift; waiting for the coming of our Lord Jesus Christ.

1 Corinthians 1:4-7

And I have filled him with the spirit of God, in wisdom, and in understanding, and in knowledge, and in all manner of workmanship.

Exodus 31:3

55

If ye abide in me, and my words abide in you, ye shall ask what ye will, and it shall be done unto you.

John 15:7

As every man hath received the gift, even so minister the same one to another, as good stewards of the manifold grace of God.

If any man speak, let him speak as the oracles of God; if any man minister, let him do it as of the ability which God giveth: that God in all things may be glorified through Jesus Christ, to whom be praise and dominion for ever and ever. Amen.

1 Peter 4:10,11

And I, behold, I have given with him Aholiab, the son of Ahisamach, of the tribe of Dan: and in the hearts of all that are wise hearted I have put wisdom, that they may make all that I have commanded thee.

Exodus 31:6

Grace and peace be multiplied unto you through the knowledge of God, and of Jesus our Lord,

According as his divine power hath given unto us all things that pertain unto life and godliness, through the knowledge of him that hath called us to glory and virtue.

2 Peter 1:2,3

Blessed be the LORD my strength, which teacheth my hands to war, and my fingers to fight.

Psalm 144:1

Abide in me, and I in you. As the branch cannot bear fruit of itself, except it abide in the vine; no more can ye, except ye abide in me.

I am the vine, ye are the branches: He that abideth in me, and I in him, the same bringeth forth much fruit: for without me ye can do nothing.

John 15:4,5

For by thee I have run through a troop; and by my God have I leaped over a wall.

Psalm 18:29

Nay, in all these things we are more than conquerors through him that loved us.

Romans 8:37

But my God shall supply all your need according to his riches in glory by Christ Jesus.

Philippians 4:19

Bible Promises for Finding Friends

Delight thyself also in the LORD; and he shall give thee the desires of thine heart.

Psalm 37:4

A man that hath friends must shew himself friendly: and there is a friend that sticketh closer than a brother.

Proverbs 18:24

A friend loveth at all times, and a brother is born for adversity.

Proverbs 17:17

He that walketh with wise men shall be wise: but a companion of fools shall be destroyed.

Proverbs 13:20

Let nothing be done through strife or vainglory; but in lowliness of mind let each esteem other better than themselves.

Look not every man on his own things, but every man also on the things of others.

Philippians 2:3,4

For the LORD God is a sun and shield: the LORD will give grace and glory: no good thing will he withhold from them that walk uprightly.

Psalm 84:11

Bible Promises for Being Comforted

And I will pray the Father, and he shall give you another Comforter, that he may abide with you for ever;

Even the Spirit of truth; whom the world cannot receive, because it seeth him not, neither knoweth him: but ye know him; for he dwelleth with you, and shall be in you.

I will not leave you comfortless: I will come to you.

John 14:16-18

Nevertheless I tell you the truth; It is expedient for you that I go away: for if I go not away, the Comforter will not come unto you; but if I depart, I will send him unto you.

John 16:7

But the Comforter, which is the Holy Ghost, whom the Father will send in my name, he shall teach you all things, and bring all things to your remembrance, whatsoever I have said unto you.

John 14:26

Wherefore comfort yourselves together, and edify one another, even as also ye do.

1 Thessalonians 5:11

Blessed be God, even the Father of our Lord Jesus Christ, the Father of mercies, and the God of all comfort;

Who comforteth us in all our tribulation, that we may be able to comfort them which are in any trouble, by the comfort wherewith we ourselves are comforted of God.

For as the sufferings of Christ abound in us, so our consolation also aboundeth by Christ.

2 Corinthians 1:3-5

And David was greatly distressed; for the people spake of stoning him, because the soul of all the people was grieved, every man for his sons and for his daughters: but David encouraged himself in the LORD his God.

1 Samuel 30:6

The eternal God is thy refuge, and underneath are the everlasting arms: and he shall thrust out the enemy from before thee; and shall say, Destroy them.

Deuteronomy 33:27

Yea, though I walk through the valley of the shadow of death, I will fear no evil: for thou art with me; thy rod and thy staff they comfort me.
Psalm 23:4

For in the time of trouble he shall hide me in his pavilion: in the secret of his tabernacle shall he hide me; he shall set me up upon a rock.

And now shall mine head be lifted up above mine enemies round about me: therefore will I offer in his tabernacle sacrifices of joy; I will sing, yea, I will sing praises unto the LORD.
Psalm 27:5,6

For his anger endureth but a moment; in his favour is life: weeping may endure for a night, but joy cometh in the morning.
Psalm 30:5

I will be glad and rejoice in thy mercy: for thou hast considered my trouble; thou hast known my soul in adversities.
Psalm 31:7

Cast thy burden upon the LORD, and he shall sustain thee: he shall never suffer the righteous to be moved.
Psalm 55:22

Thou tellest my wanderings: put thou my tears into thy bottle: are they not in thy book?

When I cry unto thee, then shall mine enemies turn back: this I know; for God is for me.

In God will I praise his word: in the LORD will I praise his word.

Psalm 56:8-10

This is my comfort in my affliction: for thy word hath quickened me.

Psalm 119:50

I remembered thy judgments of old, O LORD; and have comforted myself.

Psalm 119:52

Thy statutes have been my songs in the house of my pilgrimage.

Psalm 119:54

Bible Promises for Encouragement

Have not I commanded thee? Be strong and of a good courage; be not afraid, neither be thou dismayed: for the LORD thy God is with thee whithersoever thou goest.

Joshua 1:9

Now thanks be unto God, which always causeth us to triumph in Christ, and maketh manifest the savour of his knowledge by us in every place.

2 Corinthians 2:14

Being confident of this very thing, that he which hath begun a good work in you will perform it until the day of Jesus Christ.

Philippians 1:6

In the day when I cried thou answeredst me, and strengthenedst me with strength in my soul.

Psalm 138:3

Though I walk in the midst of trouble, thou wilt revive me: thou shalt stretch forth thine hand against the wrath of mine enemies, and thy right hand shall save me.

The LORD will perfect that which concerneth me: thy mercy, O LORD, endureth for ever: forsake not the works of thine own hands.

Psalm 138:7,8

But thou, O LORD, be merciful unto me, and raise me up, that I may requite them.

Psalm 41:10

When thou passest through the waters, I will be with thee; and through the rivers, they shall not overflow thee: when thou walkest through the fire, thou shalt not be burned; neither shall the flame kindle upon thee.

Isaiah 43:2

For the LORD shall comfort Zion: he will comfort all her waste places; and he will make her wilderness like Eden, and her desert like the garden of the LORD; joy and gladness shall be found therein, thanksgiving, and the voice of melody.

Isaiah 51:3

I, even I, am he that comforteth you: who art thou, that thou shouldest be afraid of a man that shall die, and of the son of man which shall be made as grass.

Isaiah 51:12

The LORD will perfect that which concerneth me: thy mercy, O LORD, endureth for ever: forsake not the works of thine own hands.

Psalm 138:8

For I know the thoughts that I think toward you, saith the LORD, thoughts of peace, and not of evil, to give you an expected end.

Jeremiah 29:11

Now our Lord Jesus Christ himself, and God, even our Father, which hath loved us, and hath given us everlasting consolation and good hope through grace,

Comfort your hearts, and stablish you in every good word and work.

2 Thessalonians 2:16,17

For God is not unrighteous to forget your work and labour of love, which ye have shewed toward his name, in that ye have ministered to the saints, and do minister.

And we desire that every one of you do shew the same diligence to the full assurance of hope unto the end:

That ye be not slothful, but followers of them who through faith and patience inherit the promises.

Hebrews 6:10-12

But the mercy of the LORD is from everlasting to everlasting upon them that fear him, and his righteousness unto children's children.

Psalm 103:17

Be strong and of a good courage, fear not, nor be afraid of them: for the LORD thy God, he it is that doth go with thee; he will not fail thee, nor forsake thee.

Deuteronomy 31:6

Nevertheless I am continually with thee: thou hast holden me by my right hand.

Psalm 73:23

Then he answered and spake unto me, saying, This is the word of the LORD unto Zerubbabel, saying, Not by might, nor by power, but by my spirit, saith the LORD of hosts.

Zechariah 4:6

Trust in the LORD, and do good; so shalt thou dwell in the land, and verily thou shalt be fed.

Delight thyself also in the LORD; and he shall give thee the desires of thine heart.

Commit thy way unto the LORD; trust also in him; and he shall bring it to pass.

Psalm 37:3-5

O bless our God, ye people, and make the voice of his praise to be heard:

Which holdeth our soul in life, and suffereth not our feet to be moved.

Psalm 66:8,9

I will praise the name of God with a song, and will magnify him with thanksgiving.

Psalm 69:30

The humble shall see this, and be glad: and your heart shall live that seek God.

Psalm 69:32

But the path of the just is as the shining light,
that shineth more and more unto the perfect day.

Proverbs 4:18

Bible Promises for Faith

So then faith cometh by hearing, and hearing
by the word of God.

Romans 10:17

But what saith it? The word is nigh thee, even
in thy mouth, and in thy heart: that is, the word
of faith, which we preach.

Romans 10:8

The LORD also will be a refuge for the
oppressed, a refuge in times of trouble.

And they that know thy name will put their
trust in thee: for thou, LORD, hast not forsaken
them that seek thee.

Psalm 9:9,10

It is better to trust in the LORD than to put
confidence in man.

It is better to trust in the LORD than to put
confidence in princes.

Psalm 118:8,9

As for God, his way is perfect; the word of
the LORD is tried: he is a buckler to all them that
trust in him.

2 Samuel 22:31

A Song of degrees. They that trust in the LORD shall be as mount Zion, which cannot be removed, but abideth for ever.

Psalm 125:1

My help cometh from the LORD, which made heaven and earth.

He will not suffer thy foot to be moved: he that keepeth thee will not slumber.

Behold, he that keepeth Israel shall neither slumber nor sleep.

Psalm 121:2-4

But let all those that put their trust in thee rejoice: let them ever shout for joy, because thou defendest them: let them also that love thy name be joyful in thee.

Psalm 5:11

Now the God of hope fill you with all joy and peace in believing, that ye may abound in hope, through the power of the Holy Ghost.

Romans 15:13

For this cause also thank we God without ceasing, because, when ye received the word of God which ye heard of us, ye received it not as the word of men, but as it is in truth, the word of God, which effectually worketh also in you that believe.

1 Thessalonians 2:13

Now the just shall live by faith: but if any man draw back, my soul shall have no pleasure in him.

But we are not of them who draw back unto perdition; but of them that believe to the saving of the soul.

Hebrews 10:38,39

For whatsoever is born of God overcometh the world: and this is the victory that overcometh the world, even our faith.

1 John 5:4

And the LORD, he it is that doth go before thee; he will be with thee, he will not fail thee, neither forsake thee: fear not, neither be dismayed.

Deuteronomy 31:8

And they rose early in the morning, and went forth into the wilderness of Tekoa: and as they went forth, Jehoshaphat stood and said, Hear me, O Judah, and ye inhabitants of Jerusalem; Believe in the LORD your God, so shall ye be established; believe his prophets, so shall ye prosper.

2 Chronicles 20:20

Be strong and courageous, be not afraid nor dismayed for the king of Assyria, nor for all the multitude that is with him: for there be more with us than with him:

With him is an arm of flesh; but with us is the LORD our God to help us, and to fight our battles. And the people rested themselves upon the words of Hezekiah king of Judah.

2 Chronicles 32:7,8

Fear not, O land; be glad and rejoice: for the LORD will do great things.

Joel 2:21

Behold, his soul which is lifted up is not upright in him: but the just shall live by his faith.

Habakkuk 2:4

And David said to Solomon his son, Be strong and of good courage, and do it: fear not, nor be dismayed: for the LORD God, even my God, will be with thee; he will not fail thee, nor forsake thee, until thou hast finished all the work for the service of the house of the LORD.

1 Chronicles 28:20

The LORD is my shepherd; I shall not want.

Psalm 23:1

Bible Promises for Finances

But my God shall supply all your need according to his riches in glory by Christ Jesus.
Philippians 4:19

But this I say, He which soweth sparingly shall reap also sparingly; and he which soweth bountifully shall reap also bountifully.

Every man according as he purposeth in his heart, so let him give; not grudgingly, or of necessity: for God loveth a cheerful giver.

And God is able to make all grace abound toward you; that ye, always having all sufficiency in all things, may abound to every good work:

(As it is written, He hath dispersed abroad; he hath given to the poor: his righteousness remaineth for ever.

Now he that ministereth seed to the sower both minister bread for your food, and multiply your seed sown, and increase the fruits of your righteousness.)
2 Corinthians 9:6-10

Then answered I them, and said unto them, The God of heaven, he will prosper us; therefore we his servants will arise and build: but ye have no portion, nor right, nor memorial, in Jerusalem.
Nehemiah 2:20

71

Therefore I say unto you, Take no thought for your life, what ye shall eat, or what ye shall drink; nor yet for your body, what ye shall put on. Is not the life more than meat, and the body than raiment?

Behold the fowls of the air: for they sow not, neither do they reap, nor gather into barns; yet your heavenly Father feedeth them. Are ye not much better than they?

Which of you by taking thought can add one cubit unto his stature?

And why take ye thought for raiment? Consider the lilies of the field, how they grow; they toil not, neither do they spin:

And yet I say unto you, That even Solomon in all his glory was not arrayed like one of these.

Wherefore, if God so clothe the grass of the field, which to day is, and to morrow is cast into the oven, shall he not much more clothe you, O ye of little faith?

Therefore take no thought, saying, What shall we eat? or, What shall we drink? or, Wherewithal shall we be clothed?

(For after all these things do the Gentiles seek:) for your heavenly Father knoweth that ye have need of all these things.

But seek ye first the kingdom of God, and his righteousness; and all these things shall be added unto you.

Take therefore no thought for the morrow: for the morrow shall take thought for the things of itself. Sufficient unto the day is the evil thereof.

Matthew 6:25-34

For ye know the grace of our Lord Jesus Christ, that, though he was rich, yet for your sakes he became poor, that ye through his poverty might be rich.

2 Corinthians 8:9

As it is written, He that had gathered much had nothing over; and he that had gathered little had no lack.

2 Corinthians 8:15

Let him that stole steal no more: but rather let him labour, working with his hands the thing which is good, that he may have to give to him that needeth.

Ephesians 4:28

Give, and it shall be given unto you; good measure, pressed down, and shaken together, and running over, shall men give into your bosom. For with the same measure that ye mete withal it shall be measured to you again.

Luke 6:38

Be not deceived; God is not mocked: for whatsoever a man soweth, that shall he also reap.
Galatians 6:7

I have been young, and now am old; yet have I not seen the righteous forsaken, nor his seed begging bread.

He is ever merciful, and lendeth; and his seed is blessed.
Psalm 37:25,26

Bring ye all the tithes into the storehouse, that there may be meat in mine house, and prove me now herewith, saith the LORD of hosts, if I will not open you the windows of heaven, and pour you out a blessing, that there shall not be room enough to receive it.

And I will rebuke the devourer for your sakes, and he shall not destroy the fruits of your ground; neither shall your vine cast her fruit before the time in the field, saith the LORD of hosts.

And all nations shall call you blessed: for ye shall be a delightsome land, saith the LORD of hosts.
Malachi 3:10-12

Honour the LORD with thy substance, and with the firstfruits of all thine increase:

So shall thy barns be filled with plenty, and thy presses shall burst out with new wine.

Proverbs 3:9,10

Jesus said unto him, If thou canst believe, all things are possible to him that believeth.

Mark 9:23

Cast thy bread upon the waters: for thou shalt find it after many days.

Ecclesiastes 11:1

The LORD will not suffer the soul of the righteous to famish: but he casteth away the substance of the wicked.

Proverbs 10:3

Thus saith the LORD, thy Redeemer, the Holy One of Israel; I am the LORD thy God which teacheth thee to profit, which leadeth thee by the way that thou shouldest go.

Isaiah 48:17

Bible Promises for Forgiving Others

Be ye therefore followers of God, as dear children.

And walk in love, as Christ also hath loved us, and hath given himself for us an offering and a sacrifice to God for a sweetsmelling savour.

Ephesians 5:1,2

Be ye angry, and sin not: let not the sun go down upon your wrath:

Neither give place to the devil.

Ephesians 4:26,27

And forgive us our debts, as we forgive our debtors.

Matthew 6:12

For if ye forgive men their trespasses, your heavenly Father will also forgive you:

But if ye forgive not men their trespasses, neither will your Father forgive your trespasses.

Matthew 6:14,15

Giving thanks unto the Father, which hath made us meet to be partakers of the inheritance of the saints in light:

Who hath delivered us from the power of darkness, and hath translated us into the kingdom of his dear Son:

In whom we have redemption through his blood, even the forgiveness of sins:

Who is the image of the invisible God, the firstborn of every creature:

For by him were all things created, that are in heaven, and that are in earth, visible and invisible, whether they be thrones, or dominions, or principalities, or powers: all things were created by him, and for him:

And he is before all things, and by him all things consist.

Colossians 1:12-17

Follow peace with all men, and holiness, without which no man shall see the Lord:

Looking diligently lest any man fail of the grace of God; lest any root of bitterness springing up trouble you, and thereby many be defiled.

Hebrews 12:14,15

Charity suffereth long, and is kind; charity envieth not; charity vaunteth not itself, is not puffed up,

Doth not behave itself unseemly, seeketh not her own, is not easily provoked, thinketh no evil;

Rejoiceth not in iniquity, but rejoiceth in the truth;

Beareth all things, believeth all things, hopeth all things, endureth all things.

Charity never faileth: but whether there be prophecies, they shall fail; whether there be tongues, they shall cease; whether there be knowledge, it shall vanish away.

1 Corinthians 13:4-8a

The discretion of a man deferreth his anger; and it is his glory to pass over a transgression.

Proverbs 19:11

If thou meet thine enemy's ox or his ass going astray, thou shalt surely bring it back to him again.

If thou see the ass of him that hateth thee lying under his burden, and wouldest forbear to help him, thou shalt surely help with him.

Exodus 23:4,5

Blessed are the merciful: for they shall obtain mercy.

Matthew 5:7

But I say unto you, That ye resist not evil: but whosoever shall smite thee on thy right cheek, turn to him the other also.

And if any man will sue thee at the law, and take away thy coat, let him have thy cloke also.

And whosoever shall compel thee to go a mile, go with him twain.

Give to him that asketh thee, and from him that would borrow of thee turn not thou away.

Ye have heard that it hath been said, Thou shalt love thy neighbour, and hate thine enemy.

But I say unto you, Love your enemies, bless them that curse you, do good to them that hate you, and pray for them which despitefully use you, and persecute you;

That ye may be the children of your Father which is in heaven: for he maketh his sun to rise on the evil and on the good, and sendeth rain on the just and on the unjust.

For if ye love them which love you, what reward have ye? do not even the publicans the same?

Matthew 5:39-46

And when ye stand praying, forgive, if ye have ought against any: that your Father also which is in heaven may forgive you your trespasses.

Mark 11:25

But love ye your enemies, and do good, and lend, hoping for nothing again; and your reward shall be great, and ye shall be the children of the Highest: for he is kind unto the unthankful and to the evil.

Be ye therefore merciful, as your Father also is merciful.

Judge not, and ye shall not be judged: condemn not, and ye shall not be condemned: forgive, and ye shall be forgiven.

Luke 6:35-37

Take heed to yourselves: If thy brother trespass against thee, rebuke him; and if he repent, forgive him.

And if he trespass against thee seven times in a day, and seven times in a day turn again to thee, saying, I repent; thou shalt forgive him.

Luke 17:3,4

Bless them which persecute you: bless, and curse not.

Romans 12:14

Recompense to no man evil for evil. Provide things honest in the sight of all men.

Romans 12:17

Dearly beloved, avenge not yourselves, but rather give place unto wrath: for it is written, Vengeance is mine; I will repay, saith the Lord.

Romans 12:19

Be not overcome of evil, but overcome evil with good.

Romans 21:21

And be ye kind one to another, tender-hearted, forgiving one another, even as God for Christ's sake hath forgiven you.

Ephesians 4:32

Not rendering evil for evil, or railing for railing: but contrariwise blessing; knowing that ye are thereunto called, that ye should inherit a blessing.

1 Peter 3:9

Bible Promises for Good Health

Surely he hath borne our griefs, and carried our sorrows: yet we did esteem him stricken, smitten of God, and afflicted.

But he was wounded for our transgressions, he was bruised for our iniquities: the chastisement of our peace was upon him; and with his stripes we are healed.

Isaiah 53:4,5

Christ hath redeemed us from the curse of the law, being made a curse for us: for it is written, Cursed is every one that hangeth on a tree.

Galatians 3:13

And ye shall serve the LORD your God, and he shall bless thy bread, and thy water; and I will take sickness away from the midst of thee.

There shall nothing cast their young, nor be barren, in thy land: the number of thy days I will fulfil.

Exodus 23:25,26

When the even was come, they brought unto him many that were possessed with devils: and he cast out the spirits with his word, and healed all that were sick:

That it might be fulfilled which was spoken by Esaias the prophet, saying, Himself took our infirmities, and bare our sicknesses.

Matthew 8:16,17

Who his own self bare our sins in his own body on the tree, that we, being dead to sins, should live unto righteousness: by whose stripes ye were healed.

1 Peter 2:24

And said, If thou wilt diligently hearken to the voice of the LORD thy God, and wilt do that which is right in his sight, and wilt give ear to his commandments, and keep all his statutes, I will put none of these diseases upon thee, which I have brought upon the Egyptians: for I am the LORD that healeth thee.

Exodus 15:26

There shall no evil befall thee, neither shall any plague come nigh thy dwelling.

Psalm 91:10

With long life will I satisfy him, and shew him my salvation.

Psalm 91:16

Bless the LORD, O my soul, and forget not all his benefits:

Who forgiveth all thine iniquities; who healeth all thy diseases.

Psalm 103:2,3

He sent his word, and healed them, and delivered them from their destructions.

Psalm 107:20

So shall my word be that goeth forth out of my mouth: it shall not return unto me void, but it shall accomplish that which I please, and it shall prosper in the thing whereto I sent it.

Isaiah 55:11

Every good gift and every perfect gift is from above, and cometh down from the Father of lights, with whom is no variableness, neither shadow of turning.

James 1:17

And, behold, there came a leper and worshipped him saying, Lord, if thou wilt, thou canst make me clean.

And Jesus put forth his hand, and touched him, saying, I will; be thou clean. And immediately his leprosy was cleansed.

Matthew 8:2,3

How God anointed Jesus of Nazareth with the Holy Ghost and with power: who went about doing good, and healing all that were oppressed of the devil; for God was with him.

Acts 10:38

The thief cometh not, but for to steal, and to kill, and to destroy: I am come that they might have life, and that they might have it more abundantly.

John 10:10

Jesus Christ the same yesterday, and to day, and for ever.

Hebrews 13:8

Verily, verily, I say unto you, He that believeth on me, the works that I do shall he do also; and greater works than these shall he do; because I go unto my Father.

John 14:12

Is any sick among you? let him call for the elders of the church; and let them pray over him, anointing him with oil in the name of the LORD:

And the prayer of faith shall save the sick, and the Lord shall raise him up; and if he have committed sins, they shall be forgiven him.

James 5:14,15

Beloved, I wish above all things that thou mayest prosper and be in health, even as thy soul prospereth.

3 John 1:2

Ye are of God, little children, and have overcome them: because greater is he that is in you, than he that is in the world.

1 John 4:4

For verily I say unto you, That whosoever shall say unto this mountain, Be thou removed, and be thou cast into the sea; and shall not doubt in his heart, but shall believe that those things which he saith shall come to pass; he shall have whatsoever he saith.

Therefore I say unto you, What things soever ye desire, when ye pray, believe that ye receive them, and ye shall have them.

Mark 11:23,24

Bible Promises for Joy

These things have I spoken unto you, that my joy might remain in you, and that your joy might be full.

John 15:11

I will be glad and rejoice in thee: I will sing praise to thy name, O thou most High.

Psalm 9:2

And my soul shall be joyful in the LORD: it shall rejoice in his salvation.

Psalm 35:9

The LORD is my strength and my shield; my heart trusted in him, and I am helped: therefore my heart greatly rejoiceth; and with my song will I praise him.

Psalm 28:7

Thou wilt shew me the path of life: in thy presence is fulness of joy; at thy right hand there are pleasures for evermore.

Psalm 16:11

Glory and honour are in his presence; strength and gladness are in his place.

1 Chronicles 16:27

Also that day they offered great sacrifices, and rejoiced: for God had made them rejoice with great joy: the wives also and the children rejoiced: so that the joy of Jerusalem was heard even afar off.

Nehemiah 12:43

Thou hast put gladness in my heart, more than in the time that their corn and their wine increased.

Psalm 4:7

The statutes of the LORD are right, rejoicing the heart: the commandment of the LORD is pure, enlightening the eyes.

Psalm 19:8

Wilt thou not revive us again: that thy people may rejoice in thee?

Psalm 85:6

Blessed is the people that know the joyful sound: they shall walk, O LORD, in the light of thy countenance.

In thy name shall they rejoice all the day: and in thy righteousness shall they be exalted.

Psalm 89:15,16

A Psalm of praise. Make a joyful noise unto the LORD, all ye lands.

Serve the LORD with gladness: come before his presence with singing.

Psalm 100:1,2

When the LORD turned again the captivity of Zion, we were like them that dream.

Then was our mouth filled with laughter, and our tongue with singing: then said they among the heathen, The LORD hath done great things for them.

Psalm 126:1,2

Thy words were found, and I did eat them; and thy word was unto me the joy and rejoicing of mine heart: for I am called by thy name, O LORD God of hosts.

Jeremiah 15:16

Notwithstanding in this rejoice not, that the spirits are subject unto you; but rather rejoice, because your names are written in heaven.

Luke 10:20

Thou hast made known to me the ways of life; thou shalt make me full of joy with thy countenance.

Acts 2:28

And the disciples were filled with joy, and with the Holy Ghost.

Acts 13:52

For the kingdom of God is not meat and drink; but righteousness, and peace, and joy in the Holy Ghost.

Romans 14:17

For ye were sometimes darkness, but now are ye light in the Lord: walk as children of light.

Ephesians 5:8

Those things, which ye have both learned, and received, and heard, and seen in me, do: and the God of peace shall be with you.

Philippians 4:9

Whom having not seen, ye love; in whom, though now ye see him not, yet believing, ye rejoice with joy unspeakable and full of glory.

1 Peter 1:8

Bible Promises for Love

Herein is love, not that we loved God, but that he loved us, and sent his Son to be the propitiation for our sins.

Beloved, if God so loved us, we ought also to love one another.

No man hath seen God at any time. If we love one another, God dwelleth in us, and his love is perfected in us.

1 John 4:10-12

And we have known and believed the love that God hath to us. God is love; and he that dwelleth in love dwelleth in God, and God in him.

89

Herein is our love made perfect, that we may have boldness in the day of judgment: because as he is, so are we in this world.

There is no fear in love; but perfect love casteth out fear: because fear hath torment. He that feareth is not made perfect in love.

1 John 4:16-18

And this I pray, that your love may abound yet more and more in knowledge and in all judgment;

That ye may approve things that are excellent; that ye may be sincere and without offence till the day of Christ;

Being filled with the fruits of righteousness, which are by Jesus Christ, unto the glory and praise of God.

Philippians 1:9-11

And hope maketh not ashamed; because the love of God is shed abroad in our hearts by the Holy Ghost which is given unto us.

Romans 5:5

And the Lord make you to increase and abound in love one toward another, and toward all men, even as we do toward you:

To the end he may stablish your hearts unblameable in holiness before God, even our Father, at the coming of our Lord Jesus Christ with all his saints.

1 Thessalonians 3:12,13

But as touching brotherly love ye need not that I write unto you: for ye yourselves are taught of God to love one another.

And indeed ye do it toward all the brethren which are in all Macedonia: but we beseech you, brethren, that ye increase more and more.

1 Thessalonians 4:9,10

And the Lord direct your hearts into the love of God, and into the patient waiting for Christ.

2 Thessalonians 3:5

Hatred stirreth up strifes: but love covereth all sins.

Proverbs 10:12

Set me as a seal upon thine heart, as a seal upon thine arm: for love is strong as death; jealousy is cruel as the grave: the coals thereof are coals of fire, which hath a most vehement flame.

Many waters cannot quench love, neither can the floods drown it: if a man would give all the substance of his house for love, it would utterly be contemned.

Song of Solomon 8:6,7

A friend loveth at all times, and a brother is born for adversity.

Proverbs 17:17

Honour thy father and thy mother: and, Thou shalt love thy neighbour as thyself.

Matthew 19:19

And thou shalt love the LORD thy God with all thine heart, and with all thy soul, and with all thy might.

Deuteronomy 6:5

And now, Israel, what doth the LORD thy God require of thee, but to fear the LORD thy God, to walk in all his ways, and to love him, and to serve the LORD thy God with all thy heart and with all thy soul.

Deuteronomy 10:12

But take diligent heed to do the commandment and the law, which Moses the servant of the LORD charged you, to love the LORD your

God, and to walk in all his ways, and to keep his commandments, and to cleave unto him, and to serve him with all your heart and with all your soul.

Joshua 22:5

I love the LORD, because he hath heard my voice and my supplications.

Psalm 116:1

A new commandment I give unto you, That ye love one another; as I have loved you, that ye also love one another.

By this shall all men know that ye are my disciples, if ye have love one to another.

John 13:34,35

Now as touching things offered unto idols, we know that we all have knowledge. Knowledge puffeth up, but charity edifieth.

1 Corinthians 8:1

Now the end of the commandment is charity out of a pure heart, and of a good conscience, and of faith unfeigned.

1 Timothy 1:5

And above all things have fervent charity among yourselves: for charity shall cover the multitude of sins.

1 Peter 4:8

He that loveth his brother abideth in the light, and there is none occasion of stumbling in him.

1 John 2:10

Bible Promises for Motivation

Seest thou a man diligent in his business? he shall stand before kings; he shall not stand before mean men.

Proverbs 22:29

And that ye study to be quiet, and to do your own business, and to work with your own hands, as we commanded you;

That ye may walk honestly toward them that are without, and that ye may have lack of nothing.

1 Thessalonians 4:11,12

He becometh poor that dealeth with a slack hand: but the hand of the diligent maketh rich.

Proverbs 10:4

Not slothful in business; fervent in spirit; serving the Lord.

Romans 12:11

Servants, obey in all things your masters according to the flesh; not with eyeservice, as menpleasers; but in singleness of heart, fearing God:

And whatsoever ye do, do it heartily, as to the Lord, and not unto men.

Colossians 3:22,23

And in the same house remain, eating and drinking such things as they give: for the labourer is worthy of his hire. Go not from house to house.

Luke 10:7

Wherefore I put thee in remembrance that thou stir up the gift of God, which is in thee by the putting on of my hands.

For God hath not given us the spirit of fear; but of power, and of love, and of a sound mind.

2 Timothy 1:6,7

And the people the men of Israel encouraged themselves, and set their battle again in array in the place where they put themselves in array the first day.

Judges 20:22

The hand of the diligent shall bear rule: but the slothful shall be under tribute.

Proverbs 12:24

I lead in the way of righteousness, in the midst of the paths of judgment:

That I may cause those that love me to inherit substance; and I will fill their treasures.

Proverbs 8:20,21

Slothfulness casteth into a deep sleep; and an idle soul shall suffer hunger.

Proverbs 19:15

He that gathereth in summer is a wise son: but he that sleepeth in harvest is a son that causeth shame.

Proverbs 10:5

He that tilleth his land shall be satisfied with bread: but he that followeth vain persons is void of understanding.

Proverbs 12:11

Wealth gotten by vanity shall be diminished: but he that gathereth by labour shall increase.

Proverbs 13:11

Love not sleep, lest thou come to poverty; open thine eyes, and thou shalt be satisfied with bread.

Proverbs 20:13

For even when we were with you, this we commanded you, that if any would not work, neither should he eat.

2 Thessalonians 3:10

That ye be not slothful, but followers of them who through faith and patience inherit the promises.

Hebrews 6:12

By much slothfulness the building decayeth; and through idleness of the hands the house droppeth through.

Ecclesiastes 10:18

Nay, in all these things we are more than conquerors through him that loved us.

Romans 8:37

Bible Promises for Patience

For ye have need of patience, that, after ye have done the will of God, ye might receive the promise.

Hebrews 10:36

Rest in the LORD, and wait patiently for him: fret not thyself because of him who prospereth in his way, because of the man who bringeth wicked devices to pass.

Cease from anger, and forsake wrath: fret not thyself in any wise to do evil.

For evildoers shall be cut off: but those that wait upon the LORD, they shall inherit the earth.

Psalm 37:7-9

But thou, O man of God, flee these things; and follow after righteousness, godliness, faith, love, patience, meekness.

1 Timothy 6:11

That ye be not slothful, but followers of them who through faith and patience inherit the promises.

Hebrews 6:12

Better is the end of a thing than the beginning thereof: and the patient in spirit is better than the proud in spirit.

Be not hasty in thy spirit to be angry: for anger resteth in the bosom of fools.

Ecclesiastes 7:8,9

In your patience possess ye your souls.

Luke 21:19

And not only so, but we glory in tribulations also: knowing that tribulation worketh patience.

Romans 5:3

And let us not be weary in well doing: for in due season we shall reap, if we faint not.

Galatians 6:9

I therefore, the prisoner of the Lord, beseech you that ye walk worthy of the vocation wherewith ye are called.

Ephesians 4:1

With all lowliness and meekness, with longsuffering, forbearing one another in love.

Ephesians 4:2

That ye might walk worthy of the Lord unto all pleasing, being fruitful in every good work, and increasing in the knowledge of God;

Strengthened with all might, according to his glorious power, unto all patience and longsuffering with joyfulness.

Colossians 1:10,11

Now we exhort you, brethren, warn them that are unruly, comfort the feebleminded, support the weak, be patient toward all men.

1 Thessalonians 5:14

And the Lord direct your hearts into the love of God, and into the patient waiting for Christ.

2 Thessalonians 3:5

And so, after he had patiently endured, he obtained the promise.

Hebrews 6:15

Wherefore seeing we also are compassed about with so great a cloud of witnesses, let us lay aside every weight, and the sin which doth so easily beset us, and let us run with patience the race that is set before us.

Hebrews 12:1

Knowing this, that the trying of your faith worketh patience.

But let patience have her perfect work, that ye may be perfect and entire, wanting nothing.

James 1:3,4

Wherefore, my beloved brethren, let every man be swift to hear, slow to speak, slow to wrath.

James 1:19

Be patient therefore, brethren, unto the coming of the Lord. Behold, the husbandman waiteth for the precious fruit of the earth, and hath long patience for it, until he receive the early and latter rain.

Be ye also patient; stablish your hearts: for the coming of the Lord draweth nigh.

James 5:7,8

And beside this, giving all diligence, add to your faith virtue; and to virtue knowledge;

And to knowledge temperance; and to temperance patience; and to patience godliness.

2 Peter 1:5,6

Here is the patience of the saints: here are they that keep the commandments of God, and the faith of Jesus.

Revelation 14:12

The Lord is not slack concerning his promise, as some men count slackness; but is longsuffering to us-ward, not willing that any should perish, but that all should come to repentance.

2 Peter 3:9

Bible Promises for Peace

Blessed are the peacemakers: for they shall be called the children of God.

Matthew 5:9

Thou wilt keep him in perfect peace, whose mind is stayed on thee: because he trusteth in thee.

Trust ye in the LORD for ever: for in the LORD JEHOVAH is everlasting strength.

Isaiah 26:3,4

I will hear what God the LORD will speak: for he will speak peace unto his people, and to his saints: but let them not turn again to folly.

Psalm 85:8

Now the Lord of peace himself give you peace always by all means. The Lord be with you all.
2 Thessalonians 3:16

When a man's ways please the LORD, he maketh even his enemies to be at peace with him.
Proverbs 16:7

It is an honour for a man to cease from strife: but every fool will be meddling.
Proverbs 20:3

And seek the peace of the city whither I have caused you to be carried away captives, and pray unto the LORD for it: for in the peace thereof shall ye have peace.
Jeremiah 29:7

Acquaint now thyself with him, and be at peace: thereby good shall come unto thee.
Job 22:21

When he giveth quietness, who then can make trouble? and when he hideth his face, who then can behold him? whether it be done against a nation, or against a man only.
Job 34:29

LORD, thou wilt ordain peace for us: for thou also hast wrought all our works in us.
Isaiah 26:12

What man is he that feareth the LORD? him shall he teach in the way that he shall choose.

His soul shall dwell at ease; and his seed shall inherit the earth.

Psalm 25:12,13

Mark the perfect man, and behold the upright: for the end of that man is peace.

Psalm 37:37

Great peace have they which love thy law: and nothing shall offend them.

Psalm 119:165

They that trust in the LORD shall be as mount Zion, which cannot be removed, but abideth for ever.

Psalm 125:1

To whom he said, This is the rest wherewith ye may cause the weary to rest; and this is the refreshing: yet they would not hear.

Isaiah 28:12

The glory of this latter house shall be greater than of the former, saith the LORD of hosts: and in this place will I give peace, saith the LORD of hosts.

Haggai 2:9

My covenant was with him of life and peace; and I gave them to him for the fear wherewith he feared me, and was afraid before my name.

Malachi 2:5

To give light to them that sit in darkness and in the shadow of death, to guide our feet into the way of peace.

Luke 1:79

Peace I leave with you, my peace I give unto you: not as the world giveth, give I unto you. Let not your heart be troubled, neither let it be afraid.

John 14:27

Therefore being justified by faith, we have peace with God through our Lord Jesus Christ.

Romans 5:1

For the kingdom of God is not meat and drink; but righteousness, and peace, and joy in the Holy Ghost.

Romans 14:17

Be careful for nothing; but in every thing by prayer and supplication with thanksgiving let your requests be made known unto God.

And the peace of God, which passeth all understanding, shall keep your hearts and minds through Christ Jesus.

Philippians 4:6,7

And let the peace of God rule in your hearts, to the which also ye are called in one body; and be ye thankful.

Colossians 3:15

He hath delivered my soul in peace from the battle that was against me: for there were many with me.

Psalm 55:18

Bible Promises for Protection

For this shall every one that is godly pray unto thee in a time when thou mayest be found: surely in the floods of great waters they shall not come nigh unto him.

Thou art my hiding place; thou shalt preserve me from trouble; thou shalt compass me about with songs of deliverance. Selah.

Psalm 32:6,7

He that dwelleth in the secret place of the most High shall abide under the shadow of the Almighty.

I will say of the LORD, He is my refuge and my fortress: my God; in him will I trust.

Surely he shall deliver thee from the snare of the fowler, and from the noisome pestilence.

He shall cover thee with his feathers, and under his wings shalt thou trust: his truth shall be thy shield and buckler.

Thou shalt not be afraid for the terror by night; nor for the arrow that flieth by day;

Nor for the pestilence that walketh in darkness; nor for the destruction that wasteth at noonday.

A thousand shall fall at thy side, and ten thousand at thy right hand; but it shall not come nigh thee.

Only with thine eyes shalt thou behold and see the reward of the wicked.

Because thou hast made the LORD, which is my refuge, even the most High, thy habitation;

There shall no evil befall thee, neither shall any plague come nigh thy dwelling.

For he shall give his angels charge over thee, to keep thee in all thy ways.

They shall bear thee up in their hands, lest thou dash thy foot against a stone.

Thou shalt tread upon the lion and adder: the young lion and the dragon shalt thou trample under feet.

Because he hath set his love upon me, therefore will I deliver him: I will set him on high, because he hath known my name.

He shall call upon me, and I will answer him: I will be with him in trouble; I will deliver him, and honour him.

With long life will I satisfy him, and shew him my salvation.

Psalm 91:1-16

For I, saith the LORD, will be unto her a wall of fire round about, and will be the glory in the midst of her.

Zechariah 2:5

For the which cause I also suffer these things: nevertheless I am not ashamed: for I know whom I have believed, and am persuaded that he is able to keep that which I have committed unto him against that day.

2 Timothy 1:12

God is our refuge and strength, a very present help in trouble.

Therefore will not we fear, though the earth be removed, and though the mountains be carried into the midst of the sea.

Psalm 46:1,2

God is in the midst of her; she shall not be moved: God shall help her, and that right early.

Psalm 46:5

What time I am afraid, I will trust in thee.

In God I will praise his word, in God I have put my trust; I will not fear what flesh can do unto me.

Psalm 56:3,4

Give us help from trouble: for vain is the help of man.

Through God we shall do valiantly: for he it is that shall tread down our enemies.

Psalm 60:11,12

Hear my cry, O God; attend unto my prayer.

From the end of the earth will I cry unto thee, when my heart is overwhelmed: lead me to the rock that is higher than I.

For thou hast been a shelter for me, and a strong tower from the enemy.

I will abide in thy tabernacle for ever: I will trust in the covert of thy wings. Selah.

Psalm 61:1-4

In the fear of the LORD is strong confidence: and his children shall have a place of refuge.

The fear of the LORD is a fountain of life, to depart from the snares of death.

Proverbs 14:26,27

As for God, his way is perfect; the word of the LORD is tried: he is a buckler to all them that trust in him.

2 Samuel 22:31

Now unto him that is able to keep you from falling, and to present you faultless before the presence of his glory with exceeding joy.

Jude 1:24

Bible Promises for Self-Control

This I say then, Walk in the Spirit, and ye shall not fulfil the lust of the flesh.

Galatians 5:16

Forasmuch then as Christ hath suffered for us in the flesh, arm yourselves likewise with the same mind: for he that hath suffered in the flesh hath ceased from sin;

That he no longer should live the rest of his time in the flesh to the lusts of men, but to the will of God.

1 Peter 4:1,2

Let your moderation be known unto all men. The Lord is at hand.

Philippians 4:5

Knowing this, that our old man is crucified with him, that the body of sin might be destroyed, that henceforth we should not serve sin.

Romans 6:6

But put ye on the Lord Jesus Christ, and make not provision for the flesh, to fulfil the lusts thereof.

Romans 13:14

And put a knife to thy throat, if thou be a man given to appetite.

Proverbs 23:2

He that is slow to anger is better than the mighty; and he that ruleth his spirit than he that taketh a city.

Proverbs 16:32

All things are lawful unto me, but all things are not expedient: all things are lawful for me, but I will not be brought under the power of any.

1 Corinthians 6:12

I am crucified with Christ: nevertheless I live; yet not I, but Christ liveth in me: and the life which I now live in the flesh I live by the faith of the Son of God, who loved me, and gave himself for me.

Galatians 2:20

And they that are Christ's have crucified the flesh with the affections and lusts.

Galatians 5:24

No man that warreth entangleth himself with the affairs of this life; that he may please him who hath chosen him to be a soldier.

2 Timothy 2:4

Dearly beloved, I beseech you as strangers and pilgrims, abstain from fleshly lusts, which war against the soul.

1 Peter 2:11

Hast thou found honey? eat so much as is sufficient for thee, lest thou be filled therewith, and vomit it.

Proverbs 25:16

And every man that striveth for the mastery is temperate in all things. Now they do it to obtain a corruptible crown; but we an incorruptible.

I therefore so run, not as uncertainly; so fight I, not as one that beateth the air:

But I keep under my body, and bring it into subjection: lest that by any means, when I have preached to others, I myself should be a castaway.

1 Corinthians 9:25-27

Bible Promises for Strength

The LORD is my strength and song, and he is become my salvation: he is my God, and I will prepare him an habitation; my father's God, and I will exalt him.

Exodus 15:2

He giveth power to the faint; and to them that have no might he increaseth strength.

Isaiah 40:29

Thy God hath commanded thy strength: strengthen, God, that which thou hast wrought for us.

Psalm 68:28

Finally, my brethren, be strong in the Lord, and in the power of his might.

Ephesians 6:10

God is my strength and power: And he maketh my way perfect.

2 Samuel 22:23

The LORD is my strength and song, and is become my salvation.

Psalm 118:14

Behold, God is my salvation; I will trust, and not be afraid: for the LORD JEHOVAH is my strength and my song; he also is become my salvation.

Isaiah 12:2

For thou hast girded me with strength to battle: them that rose up against me hast thou subdued under me.

2 Samuel 22:40

It is God that girdeth me with strength, and maketh my way perfect.

Psalm 18:32

112

For thou hast girded me with strength unto the battle: thou hast subdued under me those that rose up against me.

Psalm 18:39

Let the words of my mouth, and the meditation of my heart, be acceptable in thy sight, O LORD, my strength, and my redeemer.

Psalm 19:14

The LORD will give strength unto his people; the LORD will bless his people with peace.

Psalm 29:11

Sing aloud unto God our strength: make a joyful noise unto the God of Jacob.

Psalm 81:1

My flesh and my heart faileth: but God is the strength of my heart, and my portion for ever.

Psalm 73:26

A wise man is strong; yea, a man of knowledge increaseth strength.

Proverbs 24:5

Trust ye in the LORD for ever: for in the LORD JEHOVAH is everlasting strength.

Isaiah 26:4

And he said unto me, My grace is sufficient for thee: for my strength is made perfect in weakness. Most gladly therefore will I rather glory in my infirmities, that the power of Christ may rest upon me.

2 Corinthians 12:9

Bible Promises for Wisdom

If any of you lack wisdom, let him ask of God, that giveth to all men liberally, and upbraideth not; and it shall be given him.

But let him ask in faith, nothing wavering. For he that wavereth is like a wave of the sea driven with the wind and tossed.

For let not that man think that he shall receive any thing of the Lord.

A double minded man is unstable in all his ways.

James 1:5-8

For this cause we also, since the day we heard it, do not cease to pray for you, and to desire that ye might be filled with the knowledge of his will in all wisdom and spiritual understanding.

Colossians 1:9

The entrance of thy words giveth light; it giveth understanding unto the simple.

Psalm 119:130

This wisdom descendeth not from above, but is earthly, sensual, devilish.

For where envying and strife is, there is confusion and every evil work.

But the wisdom that is from above is first pure, then peaceable, gentle, and easy to be intreated, full of mercy and good fruits, without partiality, and without hypocrisy.

And the fruit of righteousness is sown in peace of them that make peace.

James 3:15-18

That the God of our Lord Jesus Christ, the Father of glory, may give unto you the spirit of wisdom and revelation in the knowledge of him:

The eyes of your understanding being enlightened; that ye may know what is the hope of his calling, and what the riches of the glory of his inheritance in the saints,

And what is the exceeding greatness of his power to us-ward who believe, according to the working of his mighty power.

Ephesians 1:17-19

He that loveth his brother abideth in the light, and there is none occasion of stumbling in him.

Call unto me, and I will answer thee, and
shew thee great and mighty things, which thou
knowest not.

Jeremiah 33:3

But ye have an unction from the Holy One,
and ye know all things.

1 John 2:20

But the anointing which ye have received of
him abideth in you, and ye need not that any
man teach you: but as the same anointing
teacheth you of all things, and is truth, and is no
lie, and even as it hath taught you, ye shall abide
in him.

1 John 2:27

And thine ears shall hear a word behind thee,
saying, This is the way, walk ye in it, when ye
turn to the right hand, and when ye turn to the
left.

Isaiah 30:21

Go not forth hastily to strive, lest thou know
not what to do in the end thereof, when thy
neighbour hath put thee to shame.

Debate thy cause with thy neighbour himself; and discover not a secret to another.

Proverbs 25:8,9

As an earring of gold, and an ornament of fine gold, so is a wise reprover upon an obedient ear.

Proverbs 25:12

I will instruct thee and teach thee in the way which thou shalt go: I will guide thee with mine eye.

Psalm 32:8

For with thee is the fountain of life: in thy light shall we see light.

Psalm 36:9

Turn you at my reproof: behold, I will pour out my spirit unto you, I will make known my words unto you.

Proverbs 1:23

For the LORD giveth wisdom: out of his mouth cometh knowledge and understanding.

He layeth up sound wisdom for the righteous: he is a buckler to them that walk uprightly.

Proverbs 2:6,7

O send out thy light and thy truth: let them lead me; let them bring me unto thy holy hill, and to thy tabernacles.

Psalm 43:3

117

Consider what I say; and the Lord give thee understanding in all things.

2 Timothy 2:7

Bible Promises for Deliverance

I sought the LORD, and he heard me, and delivered me from all my fears.

Psalm 34:4

Many are the afflictions of the righteous: but the LORD delivereth him out of them all.

Psalm 34:19

God hath spoken once; twice have I heard this; that power belongeth unto God.

Also unto thee, O Lord, belongeth mercy: for thou renderest to every man according to his work.

Psalm 62:11,12

The Lord knoweth how to deliver the godly out of temptations, and to reserve the unjust unto the day of judgment to be punished.

2 Peter 2:9

Truly my soul waiteth upon God: from him cometh my salvation.

He only is my rock and my salvation; he is my defence; I shall not be greatly moved.

Psalm 62:1,2

My soul, wait thou only upon God; for my expectation is from him.

He only is my rock and my salvation: he is my defence; I shall not be moved.

In God is my salvation and my glory: the rock of my strength, and my refuge, is in God.

Trust in him at all times; ye people, pour out your heart before him: God is a refuge for us. Selah.

Psalm 62:5-8

He sent from above, he took me, he drew me out of many waters.

He delivered me from my strong enemy, and from them which hated me: for they were too strong for me.

They prevented me in the day of my calamity: but the LORD was my stay.

He brought me forth also into a large place; he delivered me, because he delighted in me.

Psalm 18:16-19

119

Thou shalt hide them in the secret of thy presence from the pride of man: thou shalt keep them secretly in a pavilion from the strife of tongues.

Psalm 31:20

Then said Jesus to those Jews which believed on him, If ye continue in my word, then are ye my disciples indeed;

And ye shall know the truth, and the truth shall make you free.

John 8:31,32

Then he called his twelve disciples together, and gave them power and authority over all devils, and to cure diseases.

Luke 9:1

And when he had called unto him his twelve disciples, he gave them power against unclean spirits, to cast them out, and to heal all manner of sickness and all manner of disease.

Matthew 10:1

Behold, I give unto you power to tread on serpents and scorpions, and over all the power of the enemy: and nothing shall by any means hurt you.

Luke 10:19

When the even was come, they brought unto him many that were possessed with devils: and he cast out the spirits with his word, and healed all that were sick:

That it might be fulfilled which was spoken by Esaias the prophet, saying, Himself took our infirmities, and bare our sicknesses.

Matthew 8:16,17

And the Lord shall deliver me from every evil work, and will preserve me unto his heavenly kingdom: to whom be glory for ever and ever. Amen.

2 Timothy 4:18

Bible Promises for Guidance

Lead me, O LORD, in thy righteousness because of mine enemies; make thy way straight before my face.

Psalm 5:8

I will instruct thee and teach thee in the way which thou shalt go: I will guide thee with mine eye.

Psalm 32:8

For thou art my lamp, O LORD: and the LORD will lighten my darkness.

2 Samuel 22:29

Thou shalt guide me with thy counsel, and afterward receive me to glory.

Psalm 73:24

For as many as are led by the Spirit of God, they are the sons of God.

Romans 8:14

The spirit of man is the candle of the LORD, searching all the inward parts of the belly.

Proverbs 20:27

To him the porter openeth; and the sheep hear his voice: and he calleth his own sheep by name, and leadeth them out.

And when he putteth forth his own sheep, he goeth before them, and the sheep follow him: for they know his voice.

And a stranger will they not follow, but will flee from him: for they know not the voice of strangers.

John 10:3-5

Thou in thy mercy hast led forth the people which thou hast redeemed: thou hast guided them in thy strength unto thy holy habitation.

Exodus 15:13

He found him in a desert land, and in the waste howling wilderness; he led him about, he instructed him, he kept him as the apple of his eye.

Deuteronomy 32:10

Yet thou in thy manifold mercies forsookest them not in the wilderness: the pillar of the cloud departed not from them by day, to lead them in the way; neither the pillar of fire by night, to shew them light, and the way wherein they should go.

Thou gavest also thy good spirit to instruct them, and withheldest not thy manna from their mouth, and gavest them water for their thirst.

Nehemiah 9:19,20

He maketh me to lie down in green pastures: he leadeth me beside the still waters.

He restoreth my soul: he leadeth me in the paths of righteousness for his name's sake.

Psalm 23:2,3

Lead me in thy truth, and teach me: for thou art the God of my salvation; on thee do I wait all the day.

Psalm 25:5

The meek will he guide in judgment: and the meek will he teach his way.

Psalm 25:9

Teach me thy way, O LORD, and lead me in a plain path, because of mine enemies.

Psalm 27:11

For thou art my rock and my fortress; therefore for thy name's sake lead me, and guide me.

Psalm 31:3

For this God is our God for ever and ever: he will be our guide even unto death.

Psalm 48:14

From the end of the earth will I cry unto thee, when my heart is overwhelmed: lead me to the rock that is higher than I.

Psalm 61:2

If I take the wings of the morning, and dwell in the uttermost parts of the sea;

Even there shall thy hand lead me, and thy right hand shall hold me.

Psalm 139:9,10

And see if there be any wicked way in me, and lead me in the way everlasting.

Psalm 139:24

And I will bring the blind by a way that they knew not; I will lead them in paths that they have not known: I will make darkness light before them, and crooked things straight. These things will I do unto them, and not forsake them.

Isaiah 42:16

Thus saith the LORD, thy Redeemer, the Holy One of Israel; I am the LORD thy God which teacheth thee to profit, which leadeth thee by the way that thou shouldest go.

Isaiah 48:17

And the LORD shall guide thee continually, and satisfy thy soul in drought, and make fat thy bones: and thou shalt be like a watered garden, and like a spring of water, whose waters fail not.

Isaiah 58:11

To give light to them that sit in darkness and in the shadow of death, to guide our feet into the way of peace.

Luke 1:79

Howbeit when he, the Spirit of truth, is come, he will guide you into all truth: for he shall not speak of himself; but whatsoever he shall hear, that shall he speak: and he will shew you things to come.

John 16:13

Knowing this, that the trying of your faith worketh patience.

James 1:3

Call unto me, and I will answer thee, and shew thee great and mighty things, which thou knowest not.

Jeremiah 33:3

4
GOD'S PURPOSE FOR YOUR LIFE

Witnessing and Enlarging the Kingdom of God

And he said unto them, Go ye into all the world, and preach the gospel to every creature.

Mark 16:15

For I am not ashamed of the gospel of Christ: for it is the power of God unto salvation to every one that believeth; to the Jew first, and also to the Greek.

For therein is the righteousness of God revealed from faith to faith: as it is written, The just shall live by faith.

Romans 1:16,17

Now then we are ambassadors for Christ, as though God did beseech you by us: we pray you in Christ's stead, be ye reconciled to God.

2 Corinthians 5:20

And this gospel of the kingdom shall be preached in all the world for a witness unto all nations; and then shall the end come.

Matthew 24:14

Ye are the light of the world. A city that is set on an hill cannot be hid.

Neither do men light a candle, and put it under a bushel, but on a candlestick; and it giveth light unto all that are in the house.

Let your light so shine before men, that they may see your good works, and glorify your Father which is in heaven.

Matthew 5:14-16

For Christ sent me not to baptize, but to preach the gospel: not with wisdom of words, lest the cross of Christ should be made of none effect.

For the preaching of the cross is to them that perish foolishness; but unto us which are saved it is the power of God.

For it is written, I will destroy the wisdom of the wise, and will bring to nothing the understanding of the prudent.

Where is the wise? where is the scribe? where is the disputer of this world? hath not God made foolish the wisdom of this world?

For after that in the wisdom of God the world by wisdom knew not God, it pleased God by the foolishness of preaching to save them that believe.

127

For the Jews require a sign, and the Greeks seek after wisdom:

But we preach Christ crucified, unto the Jews a stumblingblock, and unto the Greeks foolishness;

But unto them which are called, both Jews and Greeks, Christ the power of God, and the wisdom of God.

Because the foolishness of God is wiser than men; and the weakness of God is stronger than men.

For ye see your calling, brethren, how that not many wise men after the flesh, not many mighty, not many noble, are called:

But God hath chosen the foolish things of the world to confound the wise; and God hath chosen the weak things of the world to confound the things which are mighty;

And base things of the world, and things which are despised, hath God chosen, yea, and things which are not, to bring to nought things that are:

That no flesh should glory in his presence.
1 Corinthians 1:17-29

And I, brethren, when I came to you, came not with excellency of speech or of wisdom, declaring unto you the testimony of God.

For I determined not to know any thing among you, save Jesus Christ, and him crucified.

And I was with you in weakness, and in fear, and in much trembling.

And my speech and my preaching was not with enticing words of man's wisdom, but in demonstration of the Spirit and of power:

That your faith should not stand in the wisdom of men, but in the power of God.

1 Corinthians 2:1-5

Now thanks be unto God, which always causeth us to triumph in Christ, and maketh manifest the savour of his knowledge by us in every place.

2 Corinthians 2:14

To the one we are the savour of death unto death; and to the other the savour of life unto life. And who is sufficient for these things?

2 Corinthians 2:16

To whom God would make known what is the riches of the glory of this mystery among the Gentiles; which is Christ in you, the hope of glory:

Whom we preach, warning every man, and teaching every man in all wisdom; that we may present every man perfect in Christ Jesus:

Whereunto I also labour, striving according to his working, which worketh in me mightily.

Colossians 1:27-29

Study to shew thyself approved unto God, a workman that needeth not to be ashamed, rightly dividing the word of truth.

2 Timothy 2:15

That ye may be blameless and harmless, the sons of God, without rebuke, in the midst of a crooked and perverse nation, among whom ye shine as lights in the world.

Philippians 2:15

Teaching them to observe all things whatsoever I have commanded you: and, lo, I am with you alway, even unto the end of the world. Amen.

Matthew 28:20

By this shall all men know that ye are my disciples, if ye have love one to another.

John 13:35

And all things are of God, who hath reconciled us to himself by Jesus Christ, and hath given to us the ministry of reconciliation.

2 Corinthians 5:18

But ye are a chosen generation, a royal priesthood, an holy nation, a peculiar people; that ye should shew forth the praises of him who hath called you out of darkness into his marvellous light.

1 Peter 2:9

The Spirit of the Lord God is upon me; because the LORD hath anointed me to preach good tidings unto the meek; he hath sent me to bind up the brokenhearted, to proclaim liberty to the captives, and the opening of the prison to them that are bound.

Isaiah 61:1

And for me, that utterance may be given unto me, that I may open my mouth boldly, to make known the mystery of the gospel.

Ephesians 6:19

For therein is the righteousness of God revealed from faith to faith: as it is written, The just shall live by faith.

Romans 1:16,17

The Bible Promises You Will Win

In whom also we have obtained an inheritance, being predestinated according to the purpose of him who worketh all things after the counsel of his own will:

That we should be to the praise of his glory, who first trusted in Christ.

Ephesians 1:11,12

And it shall come to pass afterward, that I will pour out my spirit upon all flesh; and your sons and your daughters shall prophesy, your old men shall dream dreams, your young men shall see visions:

And also upon the servants and upon the handmaids in those days will I pour out my spirit.

Joel 2:28,29

For by grace are ye saved through faith; and that not of yourselves: it is the gift of God:

Not of works, lest any man should boast.

For we are his workmanship, created in Christ Jesus unto good works, which God hath before ordained that we should walk in them.

Ephesians 2:8-10

Both young men, and maidens; old men, and children:

Let them praise the name of the LORD: for his name alone is excellent; his glory is above the earth and heaven.

Psalm 148:12,13

Let no man despise thy youth; but be thou an example of the believers, in word, in conversation, in charity, in spirit, in faith, in purity.

Till I come, give attendance to reading, to exhortation, to doctrine.

Neglect not the gift that is in thee, which was given thee by prophecy, with the laying on of the hands of the presbytery.

Meditate upon these things; give thyself wholly to them; that thy profiting may appear to all.

Take heed unto thyself, and unto the doctrine; continue in them: for in doing this thou shalt both save thyself, and them that hear thee.
1 Timothy 4:12-16

But this is that which was spoken by the prophet Joel;

And it shall come to pass in the last days, saith God, I will pour out of my Spirit upon all flesh: and your sons and your daughters shall prophesy, and your young men shall see visions, and your old men shall dream dreams:

And on my servants and on my handmaidens I will pour out in those days of my Spirit; and they shall prophesy:

Acts 2:16-18

I will stand upon my watch, and set me upon the tower, and will watch to see what he will say unto me, and what I shall answer when I am reproved.

And the LORD answered me, and said, Write the vision, and make it plain upon tables, that he may run that readeth it.

For the vision is yet for an appointed time, but at the end it shall speak, and not lie: though it tarry, wait for it; because it will surely come, it will not tarry.

Habakkuk 2:1-3

For the earth shall be filled with the knowledge of the glory of the LORD, as the waters cover the sea.

Habakkuk 2:14

I write unto you, fathers, because ye have known him that is from the beginning. I write unto you, young men, because ye have overcome the wicked one. I write unto you, little children, because ye have known the Father.

I have written unto you, fathers, because ye have known him that is from the beginning. I have written unto you, young men, because ye are strong, and the word of God abideth in you, and ye have overcome the wicked one.

Love not the world, neither the things that are in the world. If any man love the world, the love of the Father is not in him.

For all that is in the world, the lust of the flesh, and the lust of the eyes, and the pride of life, is not of the Father, but is of the world.

And the world passeth away, and the lust thereof: but he that doeth the will of God abideth for ever.

1 John 2:13-17

What Happens After Graduation?

Behold, the former things are come to pass, and new things do I declare: before they spring forth I tell you of them.

Isaiah 42:9

I will instruct thee and teach thee in the way which thou shalt go: I will guide thee with mine eye.

Psalm 32:8

Cast thy burden upon the LORD, and he shall sustain thee: he shall never suffer the righteous to be moved.

Psalm 55:22

The LORD will perfect that which concerneth me: thy mercy, O LORD, endureth for ever: forsake not the works of thine own hands.

Psalm 138:8

Commit thy works unto the LORD, and thy thoughts shall be established.

Proverbs 16:3

The simple believeth every word: but the prudent man looketh well to his going.

Proverbs 14:15

The heart of the prudent getteth knowledge; and the ear of the wise seeketh knowledge.

Proverbs 18:15

For by wise counsel thou shalt make thy war: and in multitude of counsellors there is safety.

Proverbs 24:6

And I will bring the blind by a way that they knew not; I will lead them in paths that they have not known: I will make darkness light before them, and crooked things straight. These things will I do unto them, and not forsake them.

Isaiah 42:16

Behold, I will do a new thing; now it shall spring forth; shall ye not know it? I will even make a way in the wilderness, and rivers in the desert.

Isaiah 43:19

Deciding on a College

For the LORD giveth wisdom: out of his mouth cometh knowledge and understanding.

Proverbs 2:6

Trust in the LORD with all thine heart; and lean not unto thine own understanding.

In all thy ways acknowledge him, and he shall direct thy paths.

Proverbs 3:5,6

For this cause we also, since the day we heard it, do not cease to pray for you, and to desire that ye might be filled with the knowledge of his will in all wisdom and spiritual understanding.

Colossians 1:9

If any of you lack wisdom, let him ask of God, that giveth to all men liberally, and upbraideth not; and it shall be given him.

James 1:5

I will bless the LORD, who hath given me counsel: my reins also instruct me in the night seasons.

Psalm 16:7

The entrance of thy words giveth light; it giveth understanding unto the simple.

Psalm 119:130

That the God of our Lord Jesus Christ, the Father of glory, may give unto you the spirit of wisdom and revelation in the knowledge of him:

The eyes of your understanding being enlightened; that ye may know what is the hope of his calling, and what the riches of the glory of his inheritance in the saints.

Ephesians 1:17,18

But the wisdom that is from above is first pure, then peaceable, gentle, and easy to be intreated, full of mercy and good fruits, without partiality, and without hypocrisy.

James 3:17

Choosing a Career

I will instruct thee and teach thee in the way which thou shalt go: I will guide thee with mine eye.

Psalm 32:8

Apply thine heart unto instruction, and thine ears to the words of knowledge.

Proverbs 23:12

Be strong and of a good courage, fear not, nor be afraid of them: for the LORD thy God, he it is that doth go with thee; he will not fail thee, nor forsake thee.

Deuteronomy 31:6

For thou art my lamp, O LORD: and the LORD will lighten my darkness.

2 Samuel 22:29

So teach us to number our days, that we may apply our hearts unto wisdom.

Psalm 90:12

Without counsel purposes are disappointed: but in the multitude of counsellors they are established.

Proverbs 15:22

Counsel in the heart of man is like deep water; but a man of understanding will draw it out.

Proverbs 20:5

And I will bring the blind by a way that they knew not; I will lead them in paths that they have not known: I will make darkness light before them, and crooked things straight. These things will I do unto them, and not forsake them.

Isaiah 42:16

For which of you, intending to build a tower, sitteth not down first, and counteth the cost, whether he have sufficient to finish it?

Lest haply, after he hath laid the foundation, and is not able to finish it, all that behold it begin to mock him,

Saying, This man began to build, and was not able to finish.

Luke 14:28-30

Preparing for the Future

Peace I leave with you, my peace I give unto you: not as the world giveth, give I unto you. Let not your heart be troubled, neither let it be afraid.

John 14:27

Casting all your care upon him; for he careth for you.

1 Peter 5:7

And he said, Hearken ye, all Judah, and ye inhabitants of Jerusalem, and thou king Jehoshaphat, Thus saith the LORD unto you, Be not afraid nor dismayed by reason of this great multitude; for the battle is not yours, but God's.

2 Chronicles 20:15

This book of the law shall not depart out of thy mouth; but thou shalt meditate therein day and night, that thou mayest observe to do accord-

ing to all that is written therein: for then thou
shalt make thy way prosperous, and then thou
shalt have good success.

Joshua 1:8

Commit thy works unto the LORD, and thy
thoughts shall be established.

Proverbs 16:3

Be careful for nothing; but in every thing by
prayer and supplication with thanksgiving let
your requests be made known unto God.

Philippians 4:6

Let us therefore come boldly unto the throne
of grace, that we may obtain mercy, and find
grace to help in time of need.

Hebrews 4:16

Cast not away therefore your confidence,
which hath great recompence of reward.

Hebrews 10:35

Looking for Employment

Blessed is the man that trusteth in the LORD,
and whose hope the LORD is.

Jeremiah 17:7

Thus saith the LORD, thy Redeemer, the Holy One of Israel; I am the LORD thy God which teacheth thee to profit, which leadeth thee by the way that thou shouldest go.

Isaiah 48:17

And God is able to make all grace abound toward you; that ye, always having all sufficiency in all things, may abound to every good work.

2 Corinthians 9:8

Be not ye therefore like unto them: for your Father knoweth what things ye have need of, before ye ask him.

Matthew 6:8

And the LORD, he it is that doth go before thee; he will be with thee, he will not fail thee, neither forsake thee: fear not, neither be dismayed.

Deuteronomy 31:8

The fear of man bringeth a snare: but whoso putteth his trust in the LORD shall be safe.

Proverbs 29:25

And thine ears shall hear a word behind thee, saying, This is the way, walk ye in it, when ye turn to the right hand, and when ye turn to the left.

Isaiah 30:21

Behold the fowls of the air: for they sow not, neither do they reap, nor gather into barns; yet your heavenly Father feedeth them. Are ye not much better than they?

Matthew 6:26

Jesus said unto him, If thou canst believe, all things are possible to him that believeth.

Mark 9:23

5

SCRIPTURE-BASED PRAYERS

Prayer for Yourself

Praying always with all prayer and supplication in the Spirit, and watching thereunto with all perseverance and supplication for all saints;

And for me, that utterance may be given unto me, that I may open my mouth boldly, to make known the mystery of the gospel,

For which I am an ambassador in bonds: that therein I may speak boldly, as I ought to speak.
Ephesians 6:18-20

Wherefore also we pray always for you, that our God would count you worthy of this calling, and fulfil all the good pleasure of his goodness, and the work of faith with power:

That the name of our Lord Jesus Christ may be glorified in you, and ye in him, according to the grace of our God and the Lord Jesus Christ.
2 Thessalonians 1:11,12

144

For this cause I bow my knees unto the Father of our Lord Jesus Christ,

Of whom the whole family in heaven and earth is named,

That he would grant you, according to the riches of his glory, to be strengthened with might by his Spirit in the inner man;

That Christ may dwell in your hearts by faith; that ye, being rooted and grounded in love,

May be able to comprehend with all saints what is the breadth, and length, and depth, and height;

And to know the love of Christ, which passeth knowledge, that ye might be filled with all the fulness of God.

Now unto him that is able to do exceeding abundantly above all that we ask or think, according to the power that worketh in us,

Unto him be glory in the church by Christ Jesus throughout all ages, world without end. Amen.

Ephesians 3:14-21

For this cause we also, since the day we heard it, do not cease to pray for you, and to desire that ye might be filled with the knowledge of his will in all wisdom and spiritual understanding;

That ye might walk worthy of the Lord unto all pleasing, being fruitful in every good work, and increasing in the knowledge of God;

Strengthened with all might, according to his glorious power, unto all patience and longsuffering with joyfulness;

Giving thanks unto the Father, which hath made us meet to be partakers of the inheritance of the saints in light:

Who hath delivered us from the power of darkness, and hath translated us into the kingdom of his dear Son:

In whom we have redemption through his blood, even the forgiveness of sins.

Colossians 1:9-14

That the God of our Lord Jesus Christ, the Father of glory, may give unto you the spirit of wisdom and revelation in the knowledge of him:

The eyes of your understanding being enlightened; that ye may know what is the hope of his calling, and what the riches of the glory of his inheritance in the saints,

And what is the exceeding greatness of his power to us-ward who believe, according to the working of his mighty power,

Which he wrought in Christ, when he raised him from the dead, and set him at his own right hand in the heavenly places,

Far above all principality, and power, and might, and dominion, and every name that is named, not only in this world, but also in that which is to come:

And hath put all things under his feet, and gave him to be the head over all things to the church,

Which is his body, the fulness of him that filleth all in all.

Ephesians 1:17-23

And this I pray, that your love may abound yet more and more in knowledge and in all judgment;

That ye may approve things that are excellent; that ye may be sincere and without offence till the day of Christ;

Being filled with the fruits of righteousness, which are by Jesus Christ, unto the glory and praise of God.

Philippians 1:9-11

Unto Timothy, my own son in the faith: Grace, mercy, and peace, from God our Father and Jesus Christ our Lord.

As I besought thee to abide still at Ephesus, when I went into Macedonia, that thou mightest charge some that they teach no other doctrine,

Neither give heed to fables and endless genealogies, which minister questions, rather than godly edifying which is in faith: so do.

Now the end of the commandment is charity out of a pure heart, and of a good conscience, and of faith unfeigned:

From which some having swerved have turned aside unto vain jangling.

1 Timothy 1:2-6

Making God's Word a Priority in Your Life

Thy word is a lamp unto my feet, and a light unto my path.

Psalm 119:105

This book of the law shall not depart out of thy mouth; but thou shalt meditate therein day and night, that thou mayest observe to do according to all that is written therein: for then thou shalt make thy way prosperous, and then thou shalt have good success.

Joshua 1:8

But be ye doers of the word, and not hearers only, deceiving your own selves.

James 1:22

For whatsoever things were written aforetime were written for our learning, that we through patience and comfort of the scriptures might have hope.

Romans 15:4

All scripture is given by inspiration of God, and is profitable for doctrine, for reproof, for correction, for instruction in righteousness.

2 Timothy 3:16

Heaven and earth shall pass away: but my words shall not pass away.

Mark 13:31

But he answered and said, It is written, Man shall not live by bread alone, but by every word that proceedeth out of the mouth of God.

Matthew 4:4

For the word of God is quick, and powerful, and sharper than any twoedged sword, piercing even to the dividing asunder of soul and spirit, and of the joints and marrow, and is a discerner of the thoughts and intents of the heart.

Hebrews 4:12

For the prophecy came not in old time by the will of man: but holy men of God spake as they were moved by the Holy Ghost.

2 Peter 1:21

But his delight is in the law of the LORD; and in his law doth he meditate day and night.

Psalm 1:2

Whom I have sent unto you for the same purpose, that he might know your estate, and comfort your hearts.

Colossians 4:8

He sent his word, and healed them, and delivered them from their destructions.

Psalm 107:20

As newborn babes, desire the sincere milk of the word, that ye may grow thereby.

1 Peter 2:2

Then said Jesus to those Jews which believed on him, If ye continue in my word, then are ye my disciples indeed;

And ye shall know the truth, and the truth shall make you free.

John 8:31,32

So then faith cometh by hearing, and hearing by the word of God.

Romans 10:17

But the word of the Lord endureth for ever. And this is the word which by the gospel is preached unto you.

1 Peter 1:25

Be ye mindful always of his covenant; the word which he commanded to a thousand generations.

1 Chronicles 16:15

In God I will praise his word, in God I have put my trust; I will not fear what flesh can do unto me.

Psalm 56:4

And Jesus, which is called Justus, who are of the circumcision. These only are my fellow-workers unto the kingdom of God, which have been a comfort unto me.

Colossians 4:11

Making Prayer a Priority in Your Life

And whatsoever ye shall ask in my name, that will I do, that the Father may be glorified in the Son.

If ye shall ask any thing in my name, I will do it.

John 14:13,14

Be careful for nothing; but in every thing by prayer and supplication with thanksgiving let your requests be made known unto God.

Philippians 4:6

151

For verily I say unto you, That whosoever shall say unto this mountain, Be thou removed, and be thou cast into the sea; and shall not doubt in his heart, but shall believe that those things which he saith shall come to pass; he shall have whatsoever he saith.

Therefore I say unto you, What things soever ye desire, when ye pray, believe that ye receive them, and ye shall have them.

Mark 11:23,24

Confess your faults one to another, and pray one for another, that ye may be healed. The effectual fervent prayer of a righteous man availeth much.

James 5:16

If my people, which are called by my name, shall humble themselves, and pray, and seek my face, and turn from their wicked ways; then will I hear from heaven, and will forgive their sin, and will heal their land.

2 Chronicles 7:14

When thou saidst, Seek ye my face; my heart said unto thee, Thy face, LORD, will I seek.

Psalm 27:8

Ask, and it shall be given you; seek, and ye shall find; knock, and it shall be opened unto you:

For every one that asketh receiveth; and he
that seeketh findeth; and to him that knocketh
it shall be opened.

Matthew 7:7,8

If ye abide in me, and my words abide in you,
ye shall ask what ye will, and it shall be done
unto you.

John 15:7

And in that day ye shall ask me nothing.
Verily, verily, I say unto you, Whatsoever ye shall
ask the Father in my name, he will give it you.

Hitherto have ye asked nothing in my name:
ask, and ye shall receive, that your joy may be
full.

John 16:23,24

But ye, beloved, building up yourselves on
your most holy faith, praying in the Holy Ghost.

Jude 1:20

And this is the confidence that we have in
him, that, if we ask any thing according to his
will, he heareth us:

And if we know that he hear us, whatsoever
we ask, we know that we have the petitions that
we desired of him.

1 John 5:14,15

Let us therefore come boldly unto the throne of grace, that we may obtain mercy, and find grace to help in time of need.

Hebrews 4:16

The eyes of the LORD are upon the righteous, and his ears are open unto their cry.

Psalm 34:15

Call unto me, and I will answer thee, and shew thee great and mighty things, which thou knowest not.

Jeremiah 33:3

Again I say unto you, That if two of you shall agree on earth as touching any thing that they shall ask, it shall be done for them of my Father which is in heaven.

Matthew 18:19

And all things, whatsoever ye shall ask in prayer, believing, ye shall receive.

Matthew 21:22

Part II

Prayers

6
PRAYER FOR SALVATION

Father, I pray to You and I know that I am a sinner. I need Jesus Christ in my life to save me from my sins. Thank You that You love me in spite of the type of person I have been or the things that I have done.

The Bible says that all have sinned and come short of the glory of God. It also says that my salvation is a gift from You to me. Your grace with faith is what saves me, not anything I can do or say. I confess my sins; You are faithful to forgive my sins and cleanse me from all unrighteousness and wrongful behavior. (1 John 1:9.) I turn my back on the devil and will strive to be the person that Jesus wants me to be.

Your Word says if I say with my mouth that Jesus is Lord and believe in my heart that You raised Him from the dead, I will be saved. (Rom. 10:9,10.) Jesus, I say out loud that You are the Lord of my life, and I believe that God raised You from the dead. Thank You that You are the Lord over every area of my life — my thoughts, my actions and my relationships.

Thank You, Father, for saving me! I am a new person in Jesus Christ, and heaven is my home for eternity. I recognize that I am saved by faith and not by emotion. Jesus, You are my friend, especially when I am going through hard times. As long as I stay faithful to You, no problem is too great for me.

Father, You said that I have the mind of Christ. (1 Corinthians 2:16.) I pray now for a clear mind to learn more about You. I pray that I will grow strong in my faith toward You and Your Son, Jesus. I want to know all I can about You so that I can share Your love and salvation with my friends and other people I know. Thank You, Lord, for saving me!

7
PRAYER FOR LIFE COMMITMENT

Father, there is nothing more important on this earth than knowing and obeying You. I commit myself to a lifetime of seeking and knowing You. All of this world's teachings and rules will be gone in one day, but my relationship with You will always be there. Father, I will think only about things above, things that are pleasing and worthy of You. My life is dedicated to You. I will serve You always.

God, You are an awesome and incredible Father. I have a burning desire to know You more each day; I want to live my life fully committed to You and Your ways.

In the same way that animals thirst for water, I have to have You in my life. The Bible says that those who desire and seek after You will be upright in their relationship with You, that they will always be filled with You. Father, I want to always have this hunger for truth and righteousness.

I give You my heart and commit it to You. I will always trust You. The Bible says that when I look to find You, I will find You. Father, help me look for You more every day! I love You and I know You as my God. You are protecting me as my Father. Right now I choose to love You with everything inside of me. I also choose to reach out and love others as I love myself. I commit myself to You in my youth and give You my whole heart. You are my life, and I want to obey You and please You every day of my life. Having committed myself to You, I know that You will give me the desires of my heart as Your Word says You will do.

Father, You are good to those whose hope is in You, to the one who searches for You. You are the God of heaven and earth, and You made the world and everything in it. I look for You, knowing that You are never very far. You have given me my existence, and I live my life in You. I commit my heart to You and look forward to a growing relationship with You. I give You praise!

8
PRAYER FOR A JOB

Father, in the name of Jesus I confess Your Word and the principles found in Your Word over my job search. I thank You in advance for my new job. You are the God Who teaches me how to profit and leads me in the way I should go. I trust You to lead me to the perfect job for me. You are faithful to those who love and serve You!

I ask in the name of Jesus for a job that will meet my needs. I stand fast in my faith; I walk in honesty in all situations, performing to the best of my ability, expecting prosperity. Lord, You have given me favor in the sight of all men and have increased my wisdom and position before men as a result of my obedience to and humility toward You.

I will not be afraid of compromise in any man or any situation. I have Your strength, and You will help me stand strong in honesty and integrity. I avoid all situations and men who cause trouble. I promise not to weaken in doing

161

what is right. Because of my salvation through Your Son, Jesus, I have the peace of God which brings wisdom and confidence in all situations. I am able to do any thing which is set before me.

Father, I thank You that since You are the first priority in my life, I have wisdom and direction from You. I trust in Your wisdom completely, and I am happy in Your wisdom; I will prosper and receive promotions because of it. I am prosperous and respected by many people because of You.

In my new job, I will have a drive to succeed because of Your call in my life. You have given me the strength to do anything, and I will make the best of every moment, wasting none of my time but maximizing and economizing my hours. Lord, I thank You that my inspiration and creativity come from You.

You have given me grace and favor with all men through my relationship with Your Son. I praise You for Your greatness!

9
PRAYER FOR YOUR FUTURE HUSBAND / WIFE

Father, in the name of Jesus I confess Your Word this day over my future husband/wife. I pray and ask You for a godly husband/wife. I believe that You have prepared someone for me who believes in You as I do, knows You and has the same love that I do for You. I thank You that he/she and I will be one in spirit with common goals and dreams for our lives.

I pray that my future husband/wife is not selfish or conceited, but thinks of others more highly than of himself/herself. Father, I ask that he/she considers that other people's interests are just as important as his/her own. I thank You in advance for a husband/wife who has the same servant's heart attitude that Jesus had when He was on earth.

I am glad that as my future husband/wife and I grow in our relationship, we will show the fruits of the spirit - love, joy, peace, patience, kindness, goodness, faithfulness, gentleness and self-control. My future husband/wife has the wisdom of God that helps him/her to know Your plan. He/she leads a life that is pleasing to You.

Father, I believe that You will fulfill the desires of my heart and that You always hear my prayers. I will be patient and wait for Your direction in my life. You are my hope!

(The following section is for men praying for their future wife.)

Father, I promise now that I will love my wife as Christ loves the Church. Your Word says that when I find a wife, I have found a good thing which brings favor from You. It also says that an understanding, wise and practical wife is a gift from You. Thank You that You will give me a wife who follows You and obeys Your Word. I desire only the wife who is in Your perfect will for me!

(The following section is for women praying for their future husband.)

Father, I thank You that You have a husband who is in Your perfect will for me. I commit now to love and honor my future husband. Your Word says that husbands are to love their wives as Jesus loved the Church, and I trust that my husband will be a man of Your Word. He will be pure, peaceable, gentle, merciful, and a man of integrity. Thank You, Father, that You are strengthening and perfecting my husband right now!

10
PRAYER FOR FAMILY MEMBERS

Father, I pray for patience and wisdom for my parents and family. I know that it takes hard work on both sides to make a family strong, and I pray that You will make us strong and wise. I am thankful that my parents love each other and agree on family issues.

I thank You now that all the members of my family know, or will know, Your Son, Jesus Christ, as their Lord and Savior. I ask that You help strengthen me and make me a shining light to the members of my family who are not saved. I ask that You create in them a hunger to have the relationship I have with You. Your Word says that if I delight myself in You, commit my way to You and trust in You, You will give me the desires of my heart. I desire to see the unsaved loved ones in my family come to know Jesus Christ as Lord.

I pray that I get along with my brothers and sisters and that our relationships will not be the cause of family disagreement or problems. My

165

family is like the house built on solid rock in Luke 6:48. We stand strong in our love for You and can endure and rise above any problem or situation. My family loves each other as You have asked. Your love binds us together and Your peace is in our hearts.

Father, I thank You that my parents and brothers and sisters will always choose to serve You all their lives.

PART III
MOTIVATION AND GUIDANCE

11

THE SCROLL MARKED V[1]

by
Og Mandino

I will live this day as if it is my last. And what shall I do with this last precious day which remains in my keeping? First, I will seal up its container of life so that not one drop spills itself upon the sand. I will waste not a moment mourning yesterday's misfortunes, yesterday's defeats, yesterday's aches of the heart, for why should I throw good after bad?

Can sand flow upward in the hour glass? Will the sun rise where it sets and set where it rises? Can I relive the errors of yesterday and right them? Can I call back yesterday's wounds and make them whole? Can I become younger than yesterday? Can I take back the evil that was spoken, the blows that were struck, the pain that was caused? No. Yesterday is buried forever and I will think of it no more.

I will live this day as if it is my last.

And what then shall I do? Forgetting yesterday neither will I think of tomorrow. Why should I throw *now* after *maybe*? Can tomorrow's sand flow through the glass before today's? Will the sun rise twice this morning? Can I perform tomorrow's deeds while standing in today's path? Can I place tomorrow's gold in today's purse? Can tomorrow's child be born today? Can tomorrow's death cast its shadow backward and darken today's joy? Should I torment myself with problems that may never come to pass? No! Tomorrow lies buried with yesterday, and I will think of it no more.

I will live this day as if it is my last.

This day is all I have and these hours are now my eternity. I greet this sunrise with cries of joy as a prisoner who is reprieved from death. I lift mine arms with thanks for this priceless gift of a new day. So too, I will beat upon my heart with gratitude as I consider all who greeted yesterday's sunrise who are no longer with the living today. I am indeed a fortunate man and today's hours are but a bonus, undeserved. Why have I been allowed to live this extra day when others, far better than I, have departed? Is it that they have accomplished their purpose while mine is yet to be achieved? Is this another opportunity for me to become the man I know I can be? Is there a purpose in nature? Is this my day to excel?

I will live this day as if it is my last.

I have but one life and life is naught but a measurement of time. When I waste one I destroy the other. If I waste today I destroy the last page of my life. Therefore, each hour of this day will I cherish for it can never return. It cannot be banked today to be withdrawn on the morrow, for who can trap the wind? Each minute of this day will I grasp with both hands and fondle with love for its value is beyond price. What dying man can purchase another breath though he willingly give all his gold? What price dare I place on the hours ahead? I will make them priceless!

I will live this day as if it is my last.

I will avoid with fury the killers of time. Procrastination I will destroy with action; doubt I will bury under faith; fear I will dismember with confidence. Where there are idle mouths I will listen not; where there are idle hands I will linger not; where there are idle bodies I will visit not. Henceforth I know that to court idleness is to steal food, clothing, and warmth from those I love. I am not a thief. I am a man of love and today is my last chance to prove my love and my greatness.

I will live this day as if it is my last.

The duties of today I shall fulfill today. Today I shall fondle my children while they are young; tomorrow they will be gone, and so will I. Today I shall embrace my woman with sweet kisses;

171

tomorrow she will be gone, and so will I. Today I shall lift up a friend in need; tomorrow he will no longer cry for help, nor will I hear his cries. Today I shall give myself in sacrifice and work; tomorrow I will have nothing to give, and there will be none to receive.

I will live this day as if it is my last.

And if it is my last, it will be my greatest monument. This day I will make the best day of my life. This day I will drink every minute to its full. I will savor its taste and give thanks. I will make every hour count and each minute I will trade only for something of value. I will labor harder than ever before and push my muscles until they cry for relief, and then I will continue. I will make more calls than ever before. I will sell more goods than ever before. I will earn more gold than ever before. Each minute of today will be more frutiful than hours of yesterday. My last must be my best.

I will live this day as if it is my last.

And if it is not, I shall fall to my knees and give thanks.

Endnote

This entire chapter is from *The Greatest Salesman In The World* (New York: Bantam Books, 1985) pp. 73-77. Used by permission.

12
CAUTION:
CONSTRUCTION WORK AHEAD[1]
by
Van Crouch

Where there is no vision, the people perish.
— Proverbs 29:18

The two basics for personal success are:

1) A *vision* — ''a mental sight, dream, or revelation.''

2) *A commitment to the vision.*

Exactly what is a vision?

A vision, or a goal, provides specific direction. Without a vision, you *have* no direction. To achieve, you must have an idea of what you want to achieve.

If you don't know where you are going, you will probably wind up somewhere else.[2]
— David Campbell

173

When I grew up, our home was not run like "Leave It to Beaver" or "Father Knows Best." How thankful I am today for a Christian mother who knew how to stay in the game on her knees before the Lord, praying for me. It made a tremendous difference not only in my life but in my brother's life as well.

One of the earliest examples of a vision and goal was when I got involved in high school football in my hometown of Grove City, Pennsylvania. A man named Dick Bestwick came to coach football. He became a legend. Presently he is athletic director at the University of South Carolina.

His practices were endurance contests. They were hard, hot, dirty and tough. Playing a game was almost like taking a night off. He built a tremendous winning record. More important, Bestwick and his staff worked to build character. He taught what it is to win, to be honest, to give our best. Class attendance was not optional, and respect for parents was a must.

At times, we referred to Coach Bestwick's office as a pool table. If it was necessary for him to call you in, he was likely to grab you by the shirt and bounce you off all four walls. As an educator and coach, he cared enough to confront.

As young men, we learned if we would choose to be tough on ourselves, life would be easier on us. It has always made a positive difference in my life when I have someone to be accountable to. Sound leadership will cause you to develop a vision and rise to a higher level.

Many people today, including Christians, have no vision. They do not know where they are going in life.

As I often say when I speak, the mortality rate in America is running one out of one. Everyone will die sometime.

I used to tell my prospects, "John, when they back the hearse up to the front door, they are not making a practice run!"

Therefore, it is important to make a quality decision to make the best of your life — to be the best you can, not only for Jesus, if you are a Christian, but for personal fulfillment.

Many of us run our lives as Alice did her trip through "Wonderland." If we "do not care much where" we end up, we just keep wandering around.

People with no purpose in life never get anywhere. He who expects little will not be disappointed!

Destiny is not a matter of chance; it is a matter of choice.

A goal gives you a specific direction to work toward.

Specific direction will keep you from wasting effort and time.

If your goal is to get from one city to another, you do not go off in some other direction and wander around, but proceed on course as quickly as possible. Wandering around makes you unstable, or double-minded. Then you will be like the waves of the sea, tossed to and fro, and will not receive anything when you pray. (James 1:7,8.)

Knowing your destination is half the journey.[3] In *See You at the Top*, Zig Ziglar says:

"Do most people have goals? Apparently not. You can stop a hundred young men on any street and ask each one, 'What are you doing that will absolutely guarantee your failure in life?'

"After recovering from their initial shock, each one will probably say, 'What do you mean, what am I doing to guarantee my failure? I'm working for success.'

"Tragically, most of them think they are, but...if we follow those hundred young men until they are sixty-five years old, only five of them will have achieved financial security. Only one will be wealthy. You can get better odds than that in Las Vegas. ...Do the people in life who

176

don't succeed actually plan to fail? I don't think so. The problem is they don't plan *anything*.''[4]

Happiness, wealth, and success are by-products of goal setting; they cannot be the goal themselves.[5]

Three Reasons Why Visions and Goals Are Necessary

1. They provide purpose and motivation.

2. They provide specific direction.

3. They keep you single-minded on accomplishment.

In the area of purpose and motivation, having a goal and vision to work toward, to attain, will keep you motivated. If people lose motivation and purpose, they usually die fairly quickly afterwards. Also, many times, people *die* on the inside before their bodies die. They rust out before they wear out.

When I came home from work one night, my son asked, ''Dad, what have you been doing all day?''

I said, ''Nothing much.''

He said, ''Well, how did you know when you were finished?''

My son was right! Without specific direction, you do not know which way to go nor when you

177

have arrived. Having a vision and a goal will give you that direction.

The poorest man is not he who is without a cent, but he who is without a dream.[6]
— Pennsylvania School Journal

When asked how he climbed Mt. Everest, suppose Sir Edmund Hillary replied:

''I don't know. The missus and I just went out for a walk one afternoon, and before we knew it, there we were at the top.''

Of course, that is *not* how Sir Edmund Hillary became the first man to reach the top of Mt. Everest. He had a vision: to be the first man to achieve this climb. And he had a goal: to reach the top of the mountain that had been called impossible to climb.

To achieve his vision and goal required planning, getting together supplies and equipment, finding a guide, and putting together a team. More importantly, however, it took sticking to the job at hand, persevering toward his vision and goal. Ziglar also wrote:

''Do you have a target or a goal? You must have a goal because it's just as difficult to reach a destination you don't have as it is to come back from a place where you've never been.''[7]

The Apostle Paul said in Philippians 3:14 that he was pressing on toward the mark of the high calling.

He was saying, "I keep going for the goal to fulfill the vision. I keep the goal in front of me."

A goal and vision will keep you single-minded. For example, if you need money, you should set a specific amount as a goal and a specific date by which to reach that goal. A goal cannot be set for some nebulous time in the future. It must be specific and direct, and there needs to be a deadline.

Single-mindedness is a sign of excellence because it is the single-minded person who wins. He works in a specific direction to accomplish his goal. People with a poor sense of direction in life often get lazy.

Not having a goal results in no direction, but too *many* goals result in a lack of single-mindedness. Being overextended means being tired all the time.

Inspirational Dissatisfaction

Fortunately, I was blessed with a quality I call *inspirational dissatisfaction*. Not being satisfied with where I was, I could believe in my heart there was something bigger and better and move on from there.

Charles Jones in his best-selling book, *Life Is Tremendous,* said:

"The real work is not hard work or difficult work or the actual functions that we perform, the real work is to get excited about your work and that takes work."[8]

In order to become excited about your work, you must be excited about your goal.

The greatest limitations in life are self-imposed. So go for it!

"There's no such thing as coulda, shoulda and woulda. If you shoulda and coulda, you woulda done it."

> Pat Riley
> Former coach
> of Los Angeles Lakers

A *vision* is a pictured goal.

Go For It!

The highest reward for man's toil is not what he gets for it but what he becomes by it.
> — John Ruskin

Madeline Manning Mims was born in the ghetto in Cleveland, Ohio. An inner city child, she was told she would never be able to get out of her environment.

Everything was against her.

180

But she found that she could *run* out of the ghetto when she put God on the throne of her life.

She became an Olympic Gold and Silver Medalist, qualifying for the Olympics four consecutive times over sixteen years.

In 1921 in Harlem, New York, a small boy frequently was left with relatives so his parents could go on tour with their vaudeville troupes.

His mother was mean and abusive, often venting her temper on her young son. During his childhood, he stayed with many relatives who were alcoholics. He went to eighteen different schools before he graduated from high school.

At 13, he ran away on a bicycle, heading for California hunting an aunt who lived there. When his bicycle broke down, he stole rides on freight trains, eating whatever food other hoboes left behind.

Later, he served some time in the army, then began a radio career in the late 1940s. He went on to appear on other radio shows and then television programs.

Since then, he has written two poetry anthologies, two short-story collections, several novels, and other books.

He is an accomplished musician and noted as a lyricist, having written more than four thousand songs, including scores for Broadway plays.

In addition, he is a popular lecturer, and he wrote the PBS series, "The Meeting of the Minds," a historical dramatic presentation.

But perhaps Steve Allen is best known for creating the late-night talk show format for television. The talk show he created in 1953 went on the air in 1954 as "The Tonight Show"![9]

At some time, nearly everyone must live through a storm of some kind. Perhaps it is a "broken" heart, loss of a job, breakup of a marriage. Sooner or later, adversity comes to all of us.

That is the time when we wonder if life is worth living.

We wonder, "Is the dream worth the price?"

I say, "Yes! It is."

The time when many people throw up their hands in despair, give up, and quit is the best time to *go for it.*

We look at famous people, such as Steve Allen and Madeline Mims, and say, "They made it, and I could have too *if* I had their breaks, *if* I had been in their shoes."

We think the grass is greener in our neighbors' yards.

We use our hard times as excuses to justify lack of success.

We look enviously at the successes of others, whose lives seem so glamorous.

We say, "If times weren't so tough, I could get ahead."

However, if we could take everyone's problems and put them into a big pile, then pick the ones we wanted — more than likely, we would pick our own. If we look at other people's problems, not other people's successes, our own begin to take on a new perspective.

It has been my observation over the years that 90 percent of us bring our own defeats in various ways: by too much confidence or too little, by pessimism when things look good.

This is the time to *"go for it!"*

Winners Have No Sense of Blame

The one trait common to all great and consistent winners is the absence of an attitude of blame.

They do not pout or accuse when others are at fault.

They do not rage at themselves when they are at fault.

183

Occasionally, they may be beaten — but they never "beat" themselves.

Over the long haul, they win more often than they lose, frequently by allowing their opponents to beat themselves.

I am convinced temperment more than talent or brains determines whether a person is self-fulfilling or self-destroying.

The difference between one champion and another may be trifling in terms of durability, but vast in terms of heart.

You hear a great deal about the "killer instinct" in champions. All that means, I believe, is that in the ultimate showdown, a champion forgets himself and concentrates with passionate intensity upon his object.

The near-champion never forgets himself, never subordinates himself to the goal or the game.

I do not believe the winning determination is really an instinct to "kill" or to "conquer," but an instinct for perfection, a determination to complete something started, a perfection so exquisite in itself that it obliterates the man achieving it.

A winner is beyond praise and beyond blame. He, or she, does not "beat" himself or fight himself, *but forgets himself.*

It is time in your life to put aside blame, to assume responsibility and accountability, but to put your eyes and your efforts on the goal.

Go for it!

Sow Good Seeds

Resist the temptation to accept a job based on convenience or pressure from friends or family. Pour yourself into something in which you can believe.

Do not panic or talk doubt. Refuse to be intimidated by people or circumstances. Be bold! Clothe courtesy with courage.

Do not mumble — look people in the eye when you speak. You are not a slave nor a "wimp."

Knowledge is power. The difference between failure and success is information.

There are two ways to learn:

• Experience (learning by your own mistakes), and

• Wisdom (learning from the mistakes of others).

Do not sell yourself short. Do not belittle yourself.

185

Spend time and attention on your personal growth and development. Invest in books, seminars, good clothing, and other things that will increase your confidence and sense of worth.

The better you treat yourself, the better you will be treated by others. Sow good seeds in the soil of your own life and mind.

The force, the mass of character, mind, heart, or soul that a man can put into any work, is the most important factor in that work.[10]

— A. P. Peabody

Be quick to listen.

In the insurance industry, it is said that million-dollar producers make statements while multimillion-dollar producers ask questions.

Learn *how* to listen.

Listening is an art, an ability, and an incredible tool for personal growth.

Productive listening is vital for success.

Listening demands discipline, effort, and an unselfish attitude.

Listen to those around you, especially those who are hurting.

Listen to your own conscience, the key to real success.

186

Listen for the needs of others.

Listening also is "sowing good seeds."

A wise man will hear and will increase in learning.

— Proverbs 1:5

Even a fool, when he holdeth his peace, is counted wise, and he that shutteth his lips is esteemed a man of understanding.

— Proverbs 17:28

Surround Yourself With Good People

Invest time and seek the counsel of wise people. Be a student of those who succeeded before you. Appreciate the accomplishments of others.

Absorb the wisdom of others. Do not allow their personal shortcomings to dampen your enthusiasm. Take the best, and leave the rest. Value the counsel of the learned.

He that walketh with wise men shall be wise.

— Proverbs 13:20

In a multitude of counselors there is safety.

— Proverbs 11:4

Relationships are important to success.

The most important relationship a man ever will have is with God. Spending time with God, reading His Word, communicating with Him through prayer, and letting Him communicate with you, is the best way to be victorious.

Next in importance comes your relationship with your spouse.

Third in impact upon your life are the people you choose to surround yourself with. They can make all the difference in the world.

Paul Harvey once said to me, "Van, if you want to get big fleas, hang out with big dogs!"

You should be careful who is allowed in your inner circle of friends. I do not mean to be "stand-offish," aloof, or elitist. However, you do need to make sure that the people with whom you associate the most often are in agreement with you and encourage you to move to a higher level.

Your closest friends should be people you respect, people who are diligent and conscientious. You not only will have more fun in life, but you will reach your goals quicker.

One of the most exciting things I found in the insurance industry was the "push" I got from belonging to a study group. Most of the people in the group were more advanced in the business than I was. They had more years of experience and were doing more business.

Because of the synergistic effect of the group's coming together, sharing ideas, keeping track of each other and where everyone was in production, pulled each of us up to a level where, as individuals, we would not have reached until many years later.

And the way to become truly useful is to seek the best that other brains have to offer. Use them to supplement your own, and give credit to them when they have helped.[11]

— Gordon Dean

A relationship group is not meant to be a means of letting other people do your thinking for you. Far from it! Such a group is meant to stimulate your own thinking through the association with other minds.

No one person can know everything. The more sympathetic minds — by "sympathetic," I mean those working for a common purpose — the more related information is going to be available. Great ideas usually result from a combination of related information.

You can also "surround yourself" with wise people through books, tapes, and videos.

All that mankind has done, thought, or been is lying as in magic preservation in the pages of books.[12]

— Carlyle

Winning Attitudes

Be willing to grow into greatness.

As a small acorn grows into a great oak tree, so grow the seeds of greatness within our lives:

It takes work and discipline.

It takes proper nurturing.

It takes time and may not happen overnight.

Resist impatience. As you assume responsibility for the present, take time to enjoy the things available to you right now.

Constantly hold before you the dream toward which you work.

Happiness is feeling good about yourself, and that depends very much on your productivity.

Productivity depends on your ability to set up a list of daily tasks in order of importance and accomplish them.

Avoid a complaining attitude.

Speak with enthusiasm and authority. None of us ever gets a second chance to make a first impression. Project the impression of a winner. The way you talk, dress, and act reveals much about your character. Dress neatly. Avoid the sloppiness which suggests a careless lifestyle.

190

A winner never condescends but lifts others around him to a higher level of encouragement. Help others attain their success, and you will help yourself.

Go for it!

Build a climate of confidence.

Information breeds confidence. Know *what* you believe and *why* you believe it. Disconnect the memory of past failures. Stop advertising your mistakes. Remind yourself of good decisions and triumphs of the past. See yourself winning.

Manage your time.

As I said earlier, control your time, and manage it wisely. Why? Because time is money. Treat time with the wisdom it deserves. Determine what you want to accomplish each day, each week, or each month, and set deadlines for the attainment of these goals.

Avoid time wasters — bored friends, unnecessary phone calls, idle chatter.

A day that is a social success usually is a business failure.

Be merciful.

What you make happen for others, God will make happen for you.

What you sow today determines your harvest tomorrow. Sow kindness; be slow to criticize and

191

quick to forgive. Love produces a nonjudgmental climate that will also affect you.

Become a part of someone's miracle, and it will come back to you.

Give favor and expect to receive favor. Expect others to respond favorably toward you.

Do not build mental "monsters" of fear and worry.

If a salesman expects rejection, he will multiply the possibilities and usually receive it.

Plan now for financial freedom.

Success does not "just happen." You set it in motion.

So it is with financial freedom.

You will never change where you are until you change what you are doing.

Live within your means. Do not let your upkeep be your downfall. Live with the means presently provided, and budget to correct improper and harmful spending habits.

Work hard, and be diligent, but respect your body.

Do not succumb to the "furniture disease":

That is when your chest falls into your drawers.

Health is life's first prize. Men spend their health getting wealth, then gladly pay all they have gained to get their health back!

Be good to your body. Give it sleep and proper nutrition. Exercise it, and give it the surroundings it needs. Your body is the only "machine" God will allow you during your lifetime. Value it, and take care of it.

Learn how to talk rightly, and tame your tongue.

The most powerful force in your life is your tongue. Proverbs 18:21 says, "Death and life are in the power of the tongue."

Your tongue can destroy or build, tear up or mend.

Use your words to build confidence in others. Refuse to gossip about or slander anyone else. Learn to keep confidences. To control your tongue is to control your very life.

Learn how to handle criticism.

When you decide to *go for it*, you probably will receive some.

The human heart craves acceptance and approval; rejection destroys our motivation. However, criticism can be productive or destructive, depending on how you receive it. Analyze the source, the purpose, and the solution.

Do not give any more time to a critic than you would to a friend; but, being teachable is one sign of a true winner.

Be honest.

The power of an honest life is remarkable. Integrity cannot be purchased.

There are two forces that build the gigantic machine called credibility which opens the door to success: trustworthiness and expertise.

Honesty is the hinge that swings the golden door of prosperity and success.

Never, never, never give up.

Winners are just ex-losers who got mad. The battle belongs to the persistent. The victory will go to the one who does not quit. Refuse to let friends or circumstances defeat you.

If you have been defeated, remember that from the ashes of defeat burn the greatest fires of accomplishment. Your past is the fertilizer for the future, as I said before.

God made you to climb and not crawl.

God made you to fly and not fall.

God made you to swim and not sink.

You were not made to dig in the dirt with the chickens, but to soar in the clouds with the wings of an eagle.

Go for it!

Today is *your* day.

Endnotes

[1] This entire chapter is adapted from *Stay in the Game — It's Too Soon To Quit*, (Tulsa: Honor Books, 1989) pp. 13-22, 189-207.

[2] Campbell, Dr. David. *If You Don't Know Where You're Going, You Will Probably Wind Up Somewhere Else* (Argus Communications, 1974).

[3] Carroll, Lewis. *Alice in Wonderland* (New York: Washington Square Press, Inc., 1951, 1960), p. 56.

[3] Waitley, Denis. *The Joy of Working*, (New York: Dodd, Mead & Company. Copyright © 1985 by Larimi Communications Associates, Inc.)

[4] Ziglar, Zig *See You at the Top*, (Dallas: Pelican Publishing Company. Copyright © 1975 by Zig Zigler), p. 185. Used by permission of the Pelican Publishing Co.

[5] Waitley. *Joy*, p. 39.

[6] Tan, Paul Lee. *Encyclopedia of 7700 Illustrations* (Maryland: Rockville, Assurance Publishers. Copyright © 1979 by Paul Lee Tan, ninth printing), p. 1566, Epigram.

[7] Ziglar. *See You*, p. 148.

[8] Jones, Charles. *Life Is Tremendous* (Wheaton: Tyndale House Publishers. Copyright © 1981).

[9] DeMaris, Ovid. "The Other Side of Laughter; the Pain the Gain, the Life of Steve Allen," *Parade Magazine*, pp. 4-9. Reprinted with permission from *Parade*, Copyright © May 5, 1985.

[10]*The New Dictionary,* p. 741.

[11]Quote from the late Gordon Dean, former chairman of the Atomic Energy Commission. Taken from *Sourcebook of 500 Illustrations* by Robert G. Lee, p. 100. Copyright © 1964 by Zondervan Publishing House. Used by permission.

[12]Tan. *Encyclopedia of Illustrations,* p. 215, #550.

13

PLANNING YOUR LIFE TO BE A WINNER: THE MARGIN IS JESUS[1]

by
R. Henry Migliore

1. The difference between the winner of the PGA Golf Tournament and the tenth player is an average of one stroke, the fiftieth player only four strokes. You have to be a really good golfer to even be in the top 200, but a margin of only six strokes separates the top from the 200th player.

2. In a study of aerodynamics, one learns that the leading portion of the wing provides most of an airplane's lift. Of all the square feet of space in the plane, only this very small area up and down each wing provides the margin to lift the plane.

3. The launching of the Columbia spaceship was an intricate maneuver. Everything had to be exact in terms of the centrifugal force of the earth's movement, the launching speed, and the power as the spaceship was thrust into space. The slightest margin of error on the launch would

have caused the spaceship to be off hundreds of thousands of miles as it went into orbit.

4. Everyone enjoyed the NCAA basketball championship playoff a few years ago between Georgetown and North Carolina. They played shot-for-shot and point-for-point for forty minutes. With fifteen seconds to go and Georgetown behind by one point, the final play of the game was the margin of difference between being the NCAA champion and finishing in second place.

5. If you study a football game, you will find that five or six key plays make the difference in the game. If the coaches knew which plays these would be, they would practice all week on those particular plays to be sure they are executed with perfection. The problem is that out of the eighty to one hundred plays executed, one does not know which are the key plays. This forces players to execute with precision on all of the plays so that the six or seven are executed properly. The margin for winning boils down to a very few plays.

6. The difference between winning and losing in our lives can be measured by the margin. Whenever the marginal play comes along, you will excel, and in the process, become all that you can be.

7. As much as we want to think of something as glamorous and fascinating, there is always a gritty side we have not seen. The most precious gem was once buried in dirt — and to be truly beautiful — it must be polished and cut and set in the right light. In its original state it was just as worthy, but its full potential was not known until someone recognized it and was willing and patient enough to set it free. The right amount of polishing is needed so you can realize your potential. It is not necessarily what we see on the outside that makes anyone or anything beautiful. It is that glow from the inside. There is always work to be done, a need to keep on refining, polishing, and simplifying. Every person has the opportunity to receive that inner glow, to be refined and polished. All we have to do is accept Jesus as our personal Savior. He provides the margin we need as we make our walk through life.

8. We owe it to ourselves to bring out the best of who we are — to use our talents for something beautiful — and worthy. That requires a staying power that comes only with vision and determination.

9. You need a plan to become what the Lord wants you to be. Here are the essential steps: a) have a vision / dream, b) get the facts, be aware of what is going on around you. c) analyze your strengths and weaknesses, d) make a few assump-

tions, e) set definite measurable objectives, f) be in a state of continual prayer (God will confirm, through the Holy Spirit, what is right for you), g) develop a list of strategies for each objective, h) put the plan into action, i) review progress, and j) reward yourself for accomplishment.

"Point of View"
Twenty Sure Ways To Lose Money[2]

After twenty years of helping people solve business and personal problems, I have discovered a few ways to lose one's hard-earned money. Listen carefully for these phrases, and your objective will soon be attained:

— This opportunity is available for only a short time . . . .

— You have been selected as a winner of a fabulous prize. You must . . . .

— All your friends are in on this . . . .

— You have earned the right, through your success, to be considered for . . . .

— I am a (Christian, member of a lodge or club, and so forth). Do business with me . . . .

Keep talking to the person who has this opening line and soon he will have, as the popular country song says, "the gold mine, and you will have the shaft."

Here are some rules to consider if your aim is to lose your money quickly:

1. Let someone else, preferably someone you do not know, bring you the investment idea. If they come to your door, by all means, let them in.

2. Constantly worry and plot against paying taxes. Find ways to lose so that you can deduct the losses from your taxes.

3. Be a recognized professional with your name in the yellow pages, such as a doctor or a dentist.

4. Be arrogant and have a "godlike" air.

5. Try to get rich quickly.

6. For the ultimate experience, invest money you cannot afford to lose.

7. Respond quickly with action when your mate says, "Why don't you do as well as _____?"

8. Give your mate and children credit cards and no budget.

9. Send your children to college with no accountability. Provide a car, if possible. Keep them in college no matter what.

10. Use the phone and save those letters, postcards, and stamps.

201

11. Buy raw land, the farther away from home, the better.

12. Build your wife a bigger closet.

13. Go into a business you know nothing about.

14. Do not develop a personal life plan, a financial plan, or set goals.

15. Do not buy insurance of any kind.

16. Do not make out your own personal will. Watch your loved ones from Heaven while they fight over your estate and give most of it to lawyers.

17. Get a divorce.

18. Do a lot of impulse buying.

19. Keep all your money for yourself. Do not give to your church or any worthy cause.

20. Do not ask for any advice from professionals in banking, insurance, law, investments, and accounting.

This information is meant to make all of us think before we spend. We all have most likely made some poor economic decisions and learned good lessons. Our quality of life can be affected by our economic decisions. It is to be hoped that we will be more careful and think through how we invest and spend our money.

Endnote

[1]This entire chapter is from *Personal Action Planning, How to Know What You Want and Get It* (Tulsa: Honor Books, 1988) pp. 69-71, 95-97.

Part IV
Quotes from Great Leaders

14
Words of Wisdom

The nose of the bulldog has been slanted backwards so that he can breathe without letting go.

The price of greatness is responsibility.

Winston Churchill

Nothing great will ever be achieved without great men, and men are great only if they are determined to be so.

For glory gives herself only to those who have always dreamed of her.

Charles De Gaulle

Try not to become a man of success but rather try to become a man of value.

Albert Einstein

Leadership: the art of getting someone else to do something you want done because he wants to do it.

An intellectual is a man who takes more words than necessary to tell more than he knows.

Though force can protect in emergency, only justice, fairness, consideration and cooperation can finally lead men to the dawn of eternal peace.
Dwight D. Eisenhower

Failure is only the opportunity to begin again more intelligently.

Anyone who stops learning is old, whether at twenty or eighty. Anyone who keeps learning stays young. The greatest thing in life is to keep your mind young.

My best friend is the one who brings out the best in me.

It is not the employer who pays wages — he only handles the money. It is the product that pays wages.

Don't find fault. Find a remedy.

The high wage begins down in the shop. If it is not created there it cannot get into pay envelopes. There will never be a system invented which will do away with necessity for work.
Henry Ford

Beware of little expenses. A small leak will sink a great ship.

The heart of a fool is in his mouth, but the mouth of a wise man is in his heart.

Well done is better than well said.

Benjamin Franklin

The brave man inattentive to his duty is worth little more to his country than the coward who deserts in the hour of danger.

One man with courage makes a majority.

Andrew Jackson

The most valuable of all talents is that of never using two words when one will do.

We confide in our strength, without boasting of it; we respect that of others, without fearing it.

Thomas Jefferson

A child miseducated is a child lost.

For without belittling the courage with which men have died, we should not forget those acts of courage with which men have lived.

John F. Kennedy

If a man is called to be a streetsweeper, he should sweep streets even as Michelangelo painted, or Beethoven composed music, or Shakespeare wrote poetry. He should sweep streets so well that all the hosts of heaven and earth will pause to say, here lived a great streetsweeper who did his job well.

We must use time creatively — and forever realize that the time is always hope to do great things.

Martin Luther King, Jr.

When you have got an elephant by the hind legs and he is trying to run away, it's best to let him run.

I don't think much of a man who is not wiser today than he was yesterday.

Abraham Lincoln

The quality of a person's life is in direct proportion to their commitment to excellence, regardless of their chosen field of endeavor.

It's not whether you get knocked down, it's whether you get up.

The spirit, the will to win, and the will to excel are the things that endure. These qualities are so much more important than the events that occur.

Coaches who can outline plays on a black board are a dime a dozen. The ones who win get inside their player and motivate.

Vince Lombardi

By profession I am a soldier and take pride in that fact. But I am prouder — infinitely prouder

— to be a father. A soldier destroys in order to build; the father only builds, never destroys. The one has the potentiality of death; the other embodies creation and life. And while the hordes of death are mighty, the battalions of life are mightier still. It is my hope that my son, when I am gone, will remember me not from the battle but in the home repeating with him our simple daily prayer, "Our Father Who Art in Heaven."

Douglas MacArthur

Wars may be fought with weapons, but they are won by men. It is the spirit of the men who follow and of the man who leads that gains the victory.

Never tell people how to do things. Tell them what to do and they will surprise you with their integrity.

If everyone is thinking alike then somebody isn't thinking

George Patton

The test of our progress is not whether we add more to the abundance of those who have much; it is whether we provide enough for those who have too little.

Happiness lies in the joy of achievement and the thrill of creative effort.

211

There is no indispensable man.

Franklin D. Roosevelt

I think there is only one quality worse than hardness of heart and that is softness of head.

When they call the roll in the Senate, the senators do not know whether to answer ''present'' or ''not guilty.''

The best executive is the one who has sense enough to pick good men to do what he wants done, and self-restraint enough to keep from meddling with them while they do it.

Theodore Roosevelt

Being powerful is like being a lady. If you have to tell people you are, you aren't.

Margaret Thatcher

I learned that a great leader is a man who has the ability to get other people to do what they don't want to do and like it.

It's a recession when your neighbor loses his job; it's a depression when you lose your own.

Harry S. Truman

Excellence is to do a common thing in an uncommon way.

The world cares very little about what a man or woman knows; it is what the man or woman is able to do that counts.

You can't hold a man down without staying down with him.

Booker T. Washington

Discipline is the soul of an army. It makes small numbers formidable, procures success to the weak, and esteem to all.

If the freedom of speech is taken away then dumb and silent we may be led, like sheep to the slaughter.

George Washington

Do not let what you cannot do interfere with what you can do.

Failure to prepare is preparing to fail.

Sports do not build character. They reveal it.

Be more concerned with your character than with your reputation. Your character is what you really are while your reputation is merely what others think you are.

John Wooden

No one is useless in this world who lightens the burden of it to anyone else.

Charles Dickens

Give me a stock clerk with a goal, and I will give you a man who will make history. Give me a man without a goal, and I will give you a stock clerk.

J.C. Penney

What lies behind us and what lies before us are tiny matters compared to what lies within us.

For the resolute and determined there is time and opportunity.

Ralph Waldo Emerson

In order to succeed, you must know what you are doing, like what you are doing and believe in what you are doing.

Will Rogers

Winners will take care of themselves. When you give your best effort, that is what makes you a winner.

There is no limit to what can be accomplished when no one cares who gets the credit.

John Wooden

Success . . . seems to be connected with action. Successful people keep moving. They make mistakes, but they don't quit.

Conrad Hilton

Surely a man has come to himself only when he has found the best that is in him, and has satisfied his heart with the highest achievement he is fit for.

Woodrow Wilson

You get the best out of others when you give the best of yourself.

Harvey Firestone

Destiny is not a matter of chance, it is a matter of choice.

Anonymous

The future belongs to those who believe in the beauty of their dreams.

Eleanor Roosevelt

Accept the challenges, so that you may feel that exhilaration of victory.

General George S. Patton

As I grow older, I pay less attention to what men say. I just watch what they do.

Andrew Carnegie

The credit belongs to the man who is actually in the arena, whose face is marred by dust and sweat and blood; who strives valiantly; who errs and comes short again and again, who knows the great enthusiasms, the great devotions, and spends himself in a worthy cause; who at the best, knows the triumph of high achievement; and who, at the worst, if he fails, at least fails while daring greatly, so that his place shall never be with those cold and timid souls who know neither victory nor defeat.

Theodore Roosevelt

Nothing in the world can take the place of persistence.

Talent will not; nothing is more common than unsuccessful men with talent. Genius will not; unrewarded genius is almost a proverb.

Education will not; the world is full of educated derelicts.

Persistence and determination alone are omnipotent.

Calvin Coolidge

Failure is the opportunity to begin again more intelligently.

Henry Ford

P<small>ART</small> V
31-D<small>AY</small>

DEVOTIONAL

By

John Mason

D AY 1

YOUR LEAST FAVORITE COLOR
SHOULD BE BEIGE.

Never try to defend your present position and situation. Choose to be a person who is on the offensive, not the defensive. **People who live defensively never rise above being average.** We're called, as Christians, to be on the offensive, to take the initiative. A lukewarm, indecisive person is never secure regardless of his wealth, education, or position.

Don't ever let your quest for balance become an excuse for not taking the unique, radical, invading move that God has directed you to take. Many times the attempt to maintain balance in life is really just an excuse for being lukewarm. In Joshua 1:6,7,9 the Lord says three times to Joshua, ''Be strong and courageous.'' I believe that He is saying the same thing to all believers today.

When you choose to be on the offensive, the atmosphere of your life will begin to change. So if you don't like the atmosphere of your life,

219

choose to take the offensive position. Taking the offensive is not just an action taken outside a person; it is always a decision made within.

When you do choose to be on the offensive, keep all your conflicts impersonal. Fight the issue, not the person. Speak about what God in you can do, not what others cannot do. **You will find that when all of your reasons are defensive, your cause almost never succeeds.**

Being on the offensive and taking the initiative is a master key which opens the door to opportunity in your life. Learn to create a habit of taking the initiative and **don't ever start your day in neutral.** Every morning when your feet hit the floor, you should be thinking on the offensive, reacting like an invader, taking control of your day and your life.

By pulling back and being defensive usually you enhance the problem. Intimidation always precedes defeat. If you are not sure which way to go, pray and move towards the situation in confident trust.

Be like the two fishermen who got trapped in a storm in the middle of the lake. One turned to the other and asked, ''Should we pray, or should we row?'' His wise companion responded, ''Let's do both!''

That's taking the offensive.

D~AY~ 2

GROWTH COMES FROM BUILDING ON TALENTS, GIFTS, AND STRENGTHS — NOT BY SOLVING PROBLEMS.

One of the most neglected areas in many people's lives is the area of gifts that God has placed within them. It is amazing how some people can devote their entire lives to a field of endeavor or a profession that has nothing to do with their inborn talents. In fact, the opposite is also true. Many people spend their whole lifetime trying to change who God has made them. They ignore their God-given blessings while continually seeking to change their natural makeup. As children of God, we need to recognize our innate gifts, talents, and strengths and do everything in our power to build on them.

One good thing about God's gifts and calling is that they are permanent and enduring. Romans 11:29 tells us: *...the gifts and calling of God are without repentance.* The Greek word translated *repentance* in this verse means "irrevocable." God cannot take away His gifts and calling in your life.

221

Even if you've never done anything with them, even if you've failed time and time again, God's gifts and calling are still resident within you. They are there this day, and you can choose to do something with them, beginning right now.

Gifts and talents are really God's deposits in our personal accounts, but we determine the interest on them. The greater the amount of interest and attention we give to them, the greater their value becomes. **God's gifts are never loans; they are always deposits.** As such, they are never used up or depleted. In fact, the more they are used, the greater, stronger, and more valuable they become. When they are put to good use, they provide information, insight, and revelation which cannot be received any other way or from any other source.

As Christians, we need to make full use of all the gifts and talents which God has bestowed upon us so that we do not abound in one area while becoming bankrupt in another. Someone has said, ''If the only tool you have is a hammer, you tend to treat everything like a nail.'' Don't make that mistake; use all of the gifts God has given you. If you choose not to step out and make maximum use of the gifts and talents in your life, you will spend your days on this earth helping someone else reach his goals. Most people let others control their destiny. Don't allow anyone to take over the driver's seat in your life. Fulfill your own dreams and determine your own life's course.

Never underestimate the power of the gifts that are within you. **Gifts and talents are given us to use not only so we can fulfill to the fullest the call in our own lives, but also so we can reach the souls who are attached to those gifts.** There are people whose lives are waiting to be affected by what God has placed within you. So evaluate yourself. Define and refine your gifts, talents and strengths. Choose today to look for opportunities to exercise your unique God-endowed, God-ordained gifts and calling.

Day 3

**"THE NOSE OF THE BULLDOG IS
SLANTED BACKWARDS SO HE CAN
CONTINUE TO BREATHE WITHOUT
LETTING GO."** — WINSTON CHURCHILL

Persistent people begin their success where most others quit. We Christians need to be known as people of persistence and endurance. **One person with commitment, persistence, and endurance will accomplish more than a thousand people with interest alone.** In Hebrews 12:1 (NIV) we read: *Therefore, since we are surrounded by such a great cloud of witnesses, let us throw off everything that hinders and the sin that so easily entangles, and let us run with perseverance the race marked out for us.* The more diligently we work, the harder it is to quit. Persistence is a habit; so is quitting.

Never worry about how much money, ability, or equipment you are starting with. Just begin with a million dollars worth of determination. Remember: **it's not what you have, it's what you do with what you have that makes all the**

difference. Many people eagerly begin "the good fight of faith," but they forget to add patience, persistence, and endurance to their enthusiasm. Josh Billings said: "Consider the postage stamp. Its usefulness consists in the ability to stick to something until it gets there." You and I should be known as "postage-stamp" Christians.

In First Corinthians 15:58, the Apostle Paul writes: *Therefore, my beloved brethren, be ye stedfast, unmoveable, always abounding in the work of the Lord, forasmuch as ye know that your labour is not in vain in the Lord.* Peter tells us: *Wherefore, beloved, seeing that ye look for such things, be diligent that ye may be found of him in peace, without spot, and blameless* (2 Pet. 3:14). And wise Solomon points out: *Seest thou a man diligent in his business? he shall stand before kings...*(Prov. 22:29).

In the Far East the people plant a tree called the Chinese bamboo. During the first four years they water and fertilize the plant with seemingly little or no results. Then the fifth year they again apply water and fertilizer — and in five weeks' time the tree grows ninety feet in height! The obvious question is: did the Chinese bamboo tree grow ninety feet in five weeks, or did it grow ninety feet in five years? The answer is: it grew ninety feet in five years. Because if at any time during those five years the people had stopped watering and fertilizing the tree, it would have died.

225

Many times our dreams and plans appear not to be succeeding. We are tempted to give up and quit trying. Instead, we need to continue to water and fertilize those dreams and plans, nurturing the seeds of the vision God has placed within us. Because we know that if we do not quit, if we display perseverance and endurance, we will also reap a harvest. Charles Haddon Spurgeon said, ''By perseverance the snail reached the ark.'' We need to be like that snail.

D~AY~ 4

WE CAN GROW BY OUR QUESTIONS, AS WELL AS BY OUR ANSWERS.

Here are some important questions we should ask ourselves:

1. What one decision would I make if I knew that it would not fail?

2. What one thing should I eliminate from my life because it holds me back from reaching my full potential?

3. Am I on the path of something absolutely marvelous, or something absolutely mediocre?

4. If everyone in the United States of America were on my level of spirituality, would there be a revival in the land?

5. Does the devil know who I am?

6. Am I running from something, or to something?

7. What can I do to make better use of my time?

8. Would I recognize Jesus if I met Him on the street?

9. Who do I need to forgive?

10. What is my favorite scripture for myself, my family, my career?

11. What impossible thing am I believing and planning for?

12. What is my most prevailing thought?

13. What good thing have I previously committed myself to do that I have quit doing?

14. Of the people I respect most, what is it about them that earns my respect?

15. What would a truly creative person do in my situation?

16. What outside influences are causing me to be better or worse?

17. Can I lead anyone else to Christ?

18. In what areas do I need improvement in terms of personal development?

19. What gifts, talents, or strengths do I have?

20. What is one thing that I can do for someone else who has no opportunity to repay me?

D~AY~ 5

DON'T ASK TIME WHERE IT'S GONE; TELL IT WHERE TO GO.

All great achievers, all successful people, are those who have been able to gain control over their time. It has been said that all human beings have been created equal in one respect: each person has been given 24 hours each day.

We need to choose to give our best time to our most challenging situation. It's not how much we do that matters; it's how much we get done. We should choose to watch our time, not our watch. One of the best timesavers is the ability to say no. Not saying no when you should is one of the biggest wastes of time you will ever experience.

Don't spend a dollar's worth of time for ten cent's worth of results.

Make sure to take care of the vulnerable times in your days. These vulnerable times are the first thing in the morning and the last thing at night. I have heard a minister say that what a person is like at midmight when he is all alone reveals that person's true self.

Never allow yourself to say, "I could be doing big things if I weren't so busy doing small things!" Take control of your time. **The greater control you exercise over your time, the greater freedom you will experience in your life.** The psalmist prayed, *So teach us to number our days, that we may apply our hearts unto wisdom* (Ps. 90:12). The Bible teaches us that the devil comes to steal, and to kill, and to destroy (John 10:10), and this verse applies to time as well as to people. The enemy desires to provide God's children with ideas of how to kill, steal, and destroy valuable time.

People are always saying, "I'd give anything to be able to...." There is a basic leadership principle that says, "6 x 1 = 6." If you want to write a book, learn to play a musical instrument, become a better tennis player, or do anything else important, then you should devote one hour a day, six days a week, to the project. Sooner than you think, what you desire will become reality. There are not many things that a person cannot accomplish in 312 hours a year! Just a commitment of one hour a day, six days a week, is all it takes.

We all have the same amount of time each day. The difference between people is determined by what they do with the amount of time at their disposal. Don't be like the airline pilot flying over the Pacific Ocean who reported to his passengers, "We're lost, but we're making great time!" Remember that the future arrives an hour at a time. **Gain control of your time, and you will gain control of your life**.

D<small>AY</small> 6

DON'T CONSUME YOUR TOMORROWS FEEDING ON YOUR YESTERDAYS.

Decide today to get rid of any "loser's limps" which you may still be carrying from some past experience. As followers of Jesus Christ, you and I need to break the power of the past to dominate our present and determine our future.

In Luke 9:62, Jesus said, *...No man, having put his hand to the plough, and looking back, is fit for the kingdom of God.* If we are not careful, we will allow the past to exercise a great hold on us. **The more we look backward, the less able we are to see forward.** The past makes no difference concerning what God can do for us today.

That is the beauty of the Christian life. Even when we have failed, we are able to ask for forgiveness and be totally cleansed of and released from our past actions. Whatever hold the past may have on us can be broken. It is never God Who holds us back. It is always our own choosing to allow the past to keep us from living to the fullest in the present and future. Failure is waiting around the corner for those who are living off of yesterday's successes and failures. **We should choose to be forward-focused, not past-possessed.** We should learn to profit from the past, but to invest in the future.

In Philippians 3:13,14, the Apostle Paul writes:

Brethren, I count not myself to have apprehended: but this one thing I do, forgetting those things which are behind, and reaching forth unto those things which are before,

I press toward the mark for the prize of the high calling of God in Christ Jesus.

The key here is "forgetting those things which are behind" in order to reach for "the high calling of God in Christ Jesus." To fulfill our calling in Christ, we must first forget that which lies behind. Probably the most common stronghold in a person's life is his past mistakes and failures. Today is the day to begin to shake off the shackles of the past and move forward.

The past is past. It has no life.

DAY 7

THE BEST TIME OF DAY IS NOW.

Procrastination is a killer.

When you choose to kill time, you begin to kill those gifts and callings which God has placed within your life. *The Living Bible* paraphrase of Ecclesiastes 11:4 reads: *If you wait for perfect conditions, you will never get anything done.*

The first step in overcoming procrastination is to eliminate all excuses and reasons for not taking decisive and immediate action.

Everybody is on the move. They are moving forwards, backwards, or on a treadmill. The mistake most people make is thinking that the main goal of life is to stay busy. Such thinking is a trap. What is important is not whether a person is busy, but whether he is progressing. It is a question of activity versus accomplishment.

A gentleman named John Henry Fabre conducted an experiment with processionary caterpillars. They are so named because of their

234

peculiar habit of blindly following each other no matter how they are lined up or where they are going. This man took a group of these tiny creatures and did something interesting with them. He placed them in a circle. For 24 hours the caterpillars dutifully followed one another around and around. Then he did something else. He placed the caterpillars around a saucer full of pine needles (their favorite food). For six days the mindless creatures moved around and around the saucer, literally dying from starvation and exhaustion even though an abundance of choice food was located less than two inches away.

You see, they had confused activity with accomplishment.

We Christians need to be known as those who accomplish great things for God — not those who simply talk about it. Procrastinators are good at talking versus doing. It is true what Mark Twain said: ''Noise produces nothing. Often a hen who has merely laid an egg cackles as though she has laid an asteroid.''

We need to be like the apostles. They were never known much for their policies or procedures, their theories or excuses. Instead, they were known for their acts. Many people say that they are waiting for God; but in most cases God is waiting for them. We need to say with the psalmist, ''Lord, my times are in Your hands.'' (Ps. 31:15.) The price of growth is always less

235

than the cost of stagnation. As Edmund Burke said, "The only thing necessary for the triumph of evil is for good men to do nothing."

Occasionally you may see someone who doesn't do anything, and yet seems to be successful in life. Don't be deceived. The old saying is true: "Even a broken clock is right twice a day." As Christians we are called to make progress — not excuses.

Procrastination is a primary tool of the devil to hold us back and to make us miss God's timing in our lives. *The desire of the slothful killeth him; for his hands refuse to labour* (Prov. 21:25). **The fact is, the longer we take to act on God's direction, the more unclear it becomes.**

D~AY~ 8

FEAR AND WORRY ARE INTEREST PAID IN ADVANCE ON SOMETHING YOU MAY NEVER OWN.

Fear is a poor chisel to carve out tomorrow. Worry is simply the triumph of fear over faith.

There's a story that is told about a woman who was standing on a street corner crying profusely. A man came up to her and asked why she was weeping. The lady shook her head and replied: ''I was just thinking that maybe someday I would get married. We would later have a beautiful baby girl. Then one day this child and I would go for a walk along this street, come to this corner, and my darling daughter would run into the street, get hit by a car, and die.''

Now that sounds like a pretty ridiculous situation — for a grown woman to be weeping her eyes out because of something that would probably never happen. Yet isn't this the way we respond when we worry? We take a situation or event which might never exist and build it up all out of proportion in our mind.

There is an old Swedish proverb that says, "Worry gives a small thing a big shadow." **Worry is simply the misuse of God's creative imagination which He has placed within each of us.** When fear rises in our mind, we should learn to expect the opposite in our life.

The word *worry* itself is derived from an Anglo-Saxon term meaning "to strangle," or "to choke off." There is no question that worry and fear in the mind does choke off the creative flow from above.

Things are seldom as they seem. "Skim milk masquerades as cream," said W.S. Gilbert. As we dwell on and worry about matters beyond our control, a negative effect begins to set in. Too much analysis always leads to paralysis. *Worry is a route which leads from somewhere to nowhere. Don't let it direct your life.*

In Psalm 55:22 the Bible says, *Cast thy burden upon the Lord, and he shall sustain thee: he shall never suffer the righteous to be moved.* Never respond out of fear, and never fear to respond. Action attacks fear; inaction builds fear.

Don't worry and don't fear. Instead, take your fear and worry to the Lord, *Casting all your care upon him; for he careth for you* (1 Pet. 5:7).

D~AY~ 9

OUR WORDS ARE SEEDS PLANTED INTO OTHER PEOPLE'S LIVES.

What we say is important. The Bible states that out of the abundance of the heart the mouth speaks. (Matt. 12:34.) We need to change our vocabulary. We need to speak words of life and light. Our talk should always rise to the level of the Word of God.

We Christians should be known as people who speak positively, those who speak the Word of God into situations, those who speak forth words of life.

We should not be like the man who joined a monastery in which the monks were allowed to speak only two words every seven years. After the first seven years had passed, the new initiate met with the abbot who asked him, "Well, what are your two words?"

"Food's bad," replied the man, who then went back to spend another seven-year period

239

before once again meeting with his ecclesiastical superior.

"What are your two words now?" asked the clergyman.

"Bed's hard," responded the man.

Seven years later — twenty-one years after his initial entry into the monastery — the man met with the abbot for the third and final time.

"And what are your two words this time?" he was asked.

"I quit."

"Well, I'm not surprised," answered the disgusted cleric, "all you've done since you got here is complain!"

Don't be like that man; don't be known as a person whose only words are negative.

If you are a member of the "murmuring grapevine," you need to resign. In John 6:43 our Lord instructed His disciples, ...*Murmur not among yourselves*. In Philippians 2:14,15 the Apostle Paul exhorted the believers of his day:

Do all things without murmurings and disputings:

That ye may be blameless and harmless, the sons of God, without rebuke, in the midst of a crooked and perverse nation, among whom ye shine as lights in the world.

240

Contrary to what you may have heard, talk is not cheap. Talk is very expensive. We should know that our words are powerful. What we say affects what we get from others, and what others get from us. When we speak the wrong word, it lessens our ability to see and hear the will of God.

D~AY~ 10

VERSUS.

Every day we make decisions. Daily we are confronted with options. **We must choose one or the other.** We cannot have both. These options include:

Being bitter versus being better.

Indifference versus decisiveness.

Lukewarmness versus enthusiasm.

"If we can" versus "how we can."

"Give up" versus "get up."

Security versus risk.

Coping with evil versus overcoming evil.

Blending in versus standing out.

How much we do versus how much we get done.

Coexisting with darkness versus opposing darkness.

Destruction versus development.

Resisting versus receiving.

Complaining versus obtaining.

Trying versus committing.

Peace versus strife.

Choice versus chance.

Determination versus discouragement.

Growing versus dying.

Demanding more of ourselves versus excusing ourselves.

Doing for others versus doing for self.

Progress versus regression.

Steering versus drifting.

Priorities versus aimlessness.

Accountability versus irresponsibility.

Action versus activity.

Solutions versus problems.

More of God versus more of everything else.

Being in "Who's Who" versus asking "Why me?"

D~AY~ 11

KEEP YOUR FEET ON THE ROCK WHEN YOU REACH THE END OF YOUR ROPE.

Don't quit. There is a big difference between quitting and changing. I believe that **when God sees someone who doesn't quit, He looks down and says, ''There is someone I can use.''**

In Galatians 6:9 (NIV) we are told, *Let us not become weary in doing good, for at the proper time we will reap a harvest if we do not give up.* Look at this verse carefully. It urges us not to become weary, assuring us that we will — not might — reap a harvest if we do not give up.

God doesn't quit. It is impossible for Him to do so. In Philippians 1:6 (NIV) the Apostle Paul writes about *being confident of this, that he who began a good work in you will carry it on to completion until the day of Christ Jesus.* There are several important points in this verse. The most crucial is the fact that God does not quit. Therefore, we can have great confidence that He will complete the good work He has begun in us. He will see us through every step of the way until we have reached our ultimate destination.

One of the best scriptural examples of a person who did not quit is Joseph. He had many reasons to justify giving up. First, when he was trapped in the pit into which his brothers had thrown him because of their jealousy, I am sure he said to himself, "This is not the way I dreamed my life would work out." Later on, he had a marvelous opportunity to become discouraged and quit when he was unjustly accused and thrown into prison for a crime he did not commit. Again he could have said to himself, "This is not right; I'm not supposed to be here."

But eventually the dream which God had given Joseph became reality. He was elevated from prisoner to prime minister in one day. Although Joseph did not know or understand the steps through which the Lord would lead him, he remained true to his God. Despite the trials and obstacles he faced, he did not quit.

There is no greater reward than that which comes as a result of holding fast to the Word and will of God. Only you can decide not to lose. Most people quit right on the verge of success. Often it is right at their fingertips. There is only one degree of difference between hot water and steam.

In Luke 18 (NIV) Jesus told the parable of the persistent widow. The Bible reveals His purpose in relating this story: *Then Jesus told his disciples a parable to show them they should always pray and not give up* (v. 1). The psalmist tells us, *Commit thy way unto the Lord; trust also in him; and he shall bring it to pass* (Ps. 37:5).

The only way we can lose is to quit. That is the only decision we can make that can keep us from reaching God's goals in our lives.

D~AY~ 12

A GOAL IS A DREAM WITH A DEADLINE.

In Habakkuk 2:2 the Lord tells the prophet,
*...Write the vision, and make it plain upon tables, that
he may run that readeth it*. The key to successful
goal-setting is revealed in this scripture.

First, the vision must be written down. When
you keep a vision in your mind, it is not really
a goal; it is really nothing more than a dream.
There is power in putting that dream down on
paper. When you commit something to writing,
commitment to achievement naturally follows.
You can't start a fire with paper alone, but writing
something down on paper can start a fire inside
of you.

God Himself followed His Word here, by
taking His vision for us and having it put down
on paper in the form of the Bible. He did not just
rely on the Holy Spirit to guide and direct us; He
put His goals down in writing. We are told to
make the word of the Lord plain upon ''tables''
(tablets) so that it is clear and specific as to what

247

the vision is ''...so that he may run that readeth it.''

The key word is "run." God desires that we run with the vision and goal in our life. As long as we are running with the vision, we won't turn around. When you walk with a vision, it's easy to change directions and go the wrong way. **You can't stroll to a goal.**

In Proverbs 24:3,4 (TLB), we read: *Any enterprise is built by wise planning, becomes strong through common sense, and profits wonderfully by keeping abreast of the facts.* Simply stated, effective goal-setting and planning provides an opportunity to bring the future to the present and deal with it today. You will find that achievement is easy when your outer goals become an inner commitment.

Even though we have the Holy Spirit, we still need to prepare; we are just better equipped to do so. God's first choice for us in any situation cannot be disorder and waste of funds or resources. That's why proper planning is so important. Plan to the potential. Believe for God's biggest dream. When you plan, look to the future, not the past. You can't drive forward by looking out the rear window.

Always involve yourself with something that's bigger than you are, because that's where God is. Every great success was, at the beginning, impossible. We all have opportunity for success in our lives. It takes just as much energy and effort for a bad life as it does for a good life; yet most people live meaningless lives simply because they never decided to write their vision down and then follow through on it. Know this, if you can't see the mark, you can't press towards it.

Ponder the path of thy feet, and let all thy ways be established (Prov. 4:26). You will find that what you learn on the path to your goals is actually more valuable than achieving the goal itself. Columbus discovered America while searching for a route to India. Be on the lookout for the "Americas" in your path. Put God's vision for your life on paper, and begin to run with His plan.

D~AY~ 13

SMILE — IT ADDS TO YOUR FACE VALUE.

Christians should be the happiest, most enthusiastic, people on earth. In fact, the word *enthusiasm* comes from a Greek word, *entheous* which means "God within" or "full of God."

Smiling — being happy and enthusiastic — is always a choice and not a result. It is a decision that must be consciously made. Enthusiasm and joy and happiness will improve your personality and people's opinion of you. It will help you keep a proper perspective on life. Helen Keller said, "Keep your face to the sunshine and you cannot see the shadow."

The bigger the challenge you are facing, the more enthusiasm you need. Philippians 2:5 (NIV) says, *Your attitude should be the same as that of Christ Jesus.* I believe Jesus was a man Who had a smile on His face, a spring in His step, and joy on His countenance.

Our attitude always tells others what we expect in return.

250

A smile is a powerful weapon. It can even break the ice. You'll find that being happy and enthusiastic is like a head cold — it's very, very contagious. A laugh a day will keep negative people away. You will also find that as enthusiasm increases, stress and fear in your life will decrease. The Bible says that the joy of the Lord is our strength. (Neh. 8:10.)

Many people say, "Well, no wonder that person is happy, confident, and positive; if I had his job and assets, I would be too." Such thinking falsely assumes that successful people are positive because they have a good income and lots of possessions. But the reverse is true. Such people probably have a good income and lots of possessions as a result of being positive, confident, and happy.

Enthusiasm always motivates to action. No significant accomplishment has ever been made without enthusiasm. In John 15:10,11 (NIV) we have a promise from the Lord, *"If you obey my commands, you will remain in my love, just as I have obeyed my Father's commands and remain in his love. I have told you this so that my joy may be in you and that your joy may be complete."*

The joy and love of the Lord are yours — so smile!

251

D~AY 14~

DON'T QUIT AFTER A VICTORY.

There are two times when a person stops: after a defeat and after a victory. Eliminating this kind of procrastination increases momentum.

Robert Schuller has a good saying: "Don't cash in, cast into deeper water." Don't stop after a success, keep the forward momentum going.

One of the great prizes of victory is the opportunity to do more. The trouble is, we've inoculated ourselves with small doses of success which keep us from catching the real thing.

As I was writing this section on momentum, I couldn't get out of my mind a picture of a large boulder at the top of a hill. This boulder represents our lives. If we rock the boulder back and forth and get it moving, its momentum will make it almost unstoppable. The same is true of us.

The Bible promises us God's divine momentum in our lives. In Philippians 1:6 the Apostle Paul writes, *Being confident of this very*

252

thing, that he which hath begun a good work in you will perform it until the day of Jesus Christ. God's momentum always results in growth.

There are five ways to have divine momentum in your life:

1. Be fruitful. (2 Cor. 9:10.)

2. Speak the truth. (Eph. 4:15.)

3. Be spiritually mature. (Heb. 6:1.)

4. Crave the Word of God. (1 Pet. 2:2.)

5. Grow in the grace and knowledge of Jesus. (2 Pet. 3:18.)

God's definition of spiritual momentum is found in 2 Peter 1:5 (NIV):

For this very reason, make every effort to add to your faith goodness; and to goodness, knowledge; and to knowledge, self-control; and to self-control, perseverance; and to perseverance, godliness; and to godliness, brotherly kindness; and to brotherly kindness, love. For if you possess these qualities in increasing measure, they will keep you from being ineffective and unproductive in your knowledge of our Lord Jesus Christ.

Let go of whatever makes you stop.

DAY 15

THE MOST NATURAL THING TO DO
WHEN YOU GET KNOCKED DOWN
IS TO GET UP.

How we respond to failure and mistakes is one of the most important decisions we make every day. Failure doesn't mean that nothing has been accomplished. There is always the opportunity to learn something. What is in you will always be bigger than whatever is around you.

We all experience failure and make mistakes. In fact, successful people always have more failure in their lives than average people do. You will find that throughout history all great people, at some point in their lives, have failed. **Only those who do not expect anything are never disappointed. Only those who never try, never fail.** Anyone who is currently achieving anything in life is simultaneously risking failure. It is always better to fail in doing something than to excel in doing nothing. A flawed diamond is

254

more valuable than a perfect brick. People who have no failures also have few victories.

Everybody gets knocked down, it's how fast he gets up that counts. There is a positive correlation between spiritual maturity and how quickly a person responds to his failures and mistakes. The greater the degree of spiritual maturity, the greater the ability to get back up and go on. The less the spiritual maturity, the longer the individual will continue to hang on to past failures. Every person knows someone who, to this day, is still held back by mistakes he made years ago. God never sees any of us as failures; He only sees us as learners.

We have only failed when we do not learn from the experience. The decision is up to us. We can choose to turn a failure into a hitching post, or a guidepost.

Here is the key to being free from the stranglehold of past failures and mistakes: learn the lesson and forget the details. Gain from the experience, but do not roll over and over in your mind the minute details of it. Build on the experience, and get on with your life.

Remember: **the call is higher than the fall.**

DAY 16

THOSE WHO DON'T TAKE CHANCES DON'T MAKE ADVANCES.

All great discoveries have been made by people whose faith ran ahead of their minds. Significant achievements have not been obtained by taking small risks on unimportant issues. Don't ever waste time planning, analyzing, and risking on small ideas. It is always wise to spend more time on decisions that are irreversible and less time on those that are reversible.

Learn to stretch, to reach out where God is. Aim high and take risks. The world's approach is to look to next year based on last year. We Christians need to reach to the potential, not reckon to the past. Those who make great strides are those who take chances and plan toward the challenges of life.

Don't become so caught up in small matters that you can't take advantage of important opportunities. Most people spend their entire lives letting down buckets into empty wells. They

256

continue to waste away their days trying to draw them up again.

Choose today to dream big, to strive to reach the full potential of your calling. Choose to major on the important issues of life, not on the unimportant. H. Stern said, "If you're hunting rabbits in tiger country, you must keep your eye peeled for tigers, but when you are hunting tigers you can ignore the rabbits." There are plenty of tigers to go around. Don't be distracted by or seek after the rabbits of life. Set your sights on "big game."

Security and opportunity are total strangers. If an undertaking doesn't include faith, it's not worthy of being called God's direction. I don't believe that God would call any of us to do anything that would not include an element of faith in Him.

There is a famous old saying that goes, "Even a turtle doesn't get ahead unless he sticks his neck out." **Dream big, because you serve a big God.**

D_{AY} 17

YOUR BEST FRIENDS ARE THOSE
WHO BRING OUT THE BEST IN YOU.

We need to be careful of the kind of insulation
we use in our lives. We need to insulate ourselves
from negative people and ideas. But, we should
never insulate ourselves from Godly counsel and
wisdom.

It is a fact that misery wants your company.
In Proverbs 27:19 (TLB) we read, *A mirror reflects
a man's face, but what he is really like is shown by
the kind of friends he chooses.* Proverbs 13:20 tells
us, *He that walketh with wise men shall be wise: but
a companion of fools shall be destroyed.* We become
like those with whom we associate.

Some years ago I found myself at a stagnation
point in my life. I was unproductive and unable
to see clearly God's direction. One day I noticed
that almost all of my friends were in the same
situation. When we got together, all we talked
about was our problems. As I prayed about this
matter, God showed me that He desired that I
have "foundational-level" people in my life.

258

Such people who bring out the best in us, those who influence us to become better people ourselves. They cause us to have greater faith and confidence, to see things from God's perspective. After being with them, our spirits and our sights are raised.

I have found that **it is better to be alone than in the wrong company.** A single conversation with the right person can be more valuable than many years of study.

The Lord showed me that I needed to change my closest associations, that there were some other people I needed to have contact with on a regular basis. These were men and women of great faith, those who made me a better person just by being around them. They were the ones who saw the gifts in me and could correct me in a constructive, loving way. My choice to change my closest associations was a turning point in my life.

When you surround yourself and affiliate with the right kind of people, you enter into the God-ordained power of agreement. Ecclesiastes 4:9,10,12 (TLB) states:

Two can accomplish more than twice as much as one, for the results can be much better. If one falls, the other pulls him up; but if a man falls when he is alone, he's in trouble.

And one standing alone can be attacked and defeated, but two can stand back-to-back and conquer; three is even better, for a triple-braided cord is not easily broken.

You need to steer clear of negative-thinking "experts." **Remember: in the eyes of average people average is always considered outstanding.** Look carefully at the closest associations in your life, for that is the direction you are heading.

DAY 18

WE ARE CALLED TO STAND OUT, NOT BLEND IN.

A majority, many times, is a group of highly motivated snails. If a thousand people say something foolish, it's still foolish. Truth is never dependent upon consensus of opinion.

In 1 Peter 2:9, the Bible says of us Christians, *...ye are a chosen generation, a royal priesthood, an holy nation, a peculiar people; that ye should shew forth the praises of him who hath called you out of darkness into his marvellous light.*

Romans 12:2 exhorts us, *And be not conformed to this world, but be ye transformed by the renewing of your mind, that ye may prove what is that good, and acceptable, and perfect, will of God.*

One of the greatest compliments that anybody can give you is to say that you are different. We Christians live in this world, but we are aliens. We should talk differently, act differently, and perform differently. We are called to stand out.

There should be something different about you. If you don't stand out in a group, if there is not something unique or different in your life, you should re-evaluate yourself.

One way to stand head and shoulders above the crowd is to choose to do regular, ordinary things in an extraordinary and supernatural way with great enthusiasm. God has always done some of His very best work through remnants, when the circumstances appear to be stacked against them. In fact, in every battle described in the Bible, God was always on the side of the "underdog," the minority.

Majority rule is not always right. It is usually those people who don't have dreams or visions of their own who want to take a vote. People in groups tend to agree on courses of action that they as individuals know are not right.

Don't be persuaded or dissuaded by group opinion. It doesn't make any difference whether anyone else believes, you must believe. **Never take direction from a crowd for your personal life. And never choose to quit just because somebody else disagrees with you.** In fact, the two worst things you can say to yourself when you get an idea is: 1) "That has never been done before," and 2) "That has been done before." Just because somebody else has gone a particular way and not succeeded does not mean that you too will fail.

Be a pioneer, catch a few arrows, and stand out.

DAY 19

SAY NO TO MANY GOOD IDEAS.

One of the tricks of the devil is to get us to say yes to too many things. Then we end up being spread so thin that we are mediocre in everything and excellent in nothing.

There is one guaranteed formula for failure, and that is to try to please everyone.

There is a difference between something that is good and something that is right. Oftentimes, it is a challenge for many people to discern that which is good from that which is right. As Christians, our higher responsibility is always to do the right things. These come first. We should do the things that we're called to do, the things that are right, with excellence, first — before we start diversifying into other areas.

There comes a time in every person's life when he must learn to say no to many good ideas. In fact, the more an individual grows, the more opportunities he will have to say no. Becoming focused is a key to results. Perhaps no other virtue is so overlooked as a key to growth and success. The temptation is always to do a little bit of everything.

Saying no to a good idea doesn't always mean never. No may mean not right now.

There is power in the word *no*. No is an anointed word, one which can break the yoke of overcommitment and weakness. No can be used to turn a situation from bad to good, from wrong to right. Saying no can free you from burdens that you really don't need to carry right now.

It can also allow you to devote the correct amount of attention and effort to God's priorities in your life.

I'm sure that as you read the title of this nugget, past experiences and present situations come to mind. I'm sure you recall many situations in which no or not right now would have been the right answer. Don't put yourself through that kind of disappointment in the future.

Yes and no are the two most important words that you will ever say. These are the two words that determine your destiny in life. How and when you say them affects your entire future.

Saying no to lesser things can mean saying yes to the priorities in your life.

DAY 20

WHEN YOU REFUSE TO CHANGE, YOU END UP IN CHAINS.

We humans are custom-built for change.

Inanimate objects like clothes, houses, and buildings don't have the ability to truly change. They grow out of style and become unusable. But at any point in time, at any age, any one of us is able to change. To change doesn't always mean to do the opposite. In fact, most of the time, it means to add on to or slightly adjust.

When we are called upon by the Lord to change, we will continue to reach toward the same goal, but perhaps in a slightly different way. When we refuse to cooperate with the change that God is requiring of us, we make chains that constrain and restrict us.

There are three things that we know about the future: 1) it is not going to be like the past, 2) it is not going to be exactly the way we think it's going to be, and 3) the rate of change will take place faster than we imagine. The Bible indicates that in the end times in which we are now living, changes will come about much quicker than ever before in history.

In 1803 the British created a civil service position in which a man was required to stand on the cliffs of Dover with a spy glass. His job was to be on the lookout for invasion. He was to ring a bell if he saw the army of Napoleon Bonaparte approaching. Now that was all well and good for the time, but that job was not eliminated until 1945! How many spy glasses on the cliffs of Dover are we still holding onto in our lives? **We should choose not to allow "the way we've always done it" to cause us to miss opportunities God is providing for us today.**

Even the most precious of all gems needs to be chiseled and faceted to achieve its best luster. There is nothing that remains so constant as change. Don't end up like concrete, all mixed up and permanently set.

In Isaiah 42:9, the Lord declares: *Behold, the former things are come to pass, and new things do I declare: before they spring forth I tell you of them.* The Bible is a book that tells us how to respond to change ahead of time. You see, I believe that we can decide in advance how we will respond to most situations. When I was coaching basketball many years ago, I used to tell my players that most situations in a game can be prepared for ahead of time. We used to practice different game situations so that when the players got into an actual game situation they would know how to respond. **One of the main reasons the Bible was written was to prepare us ahead of time, to teach us how to respond in advance to many of the situations that we will encounter in life.**

Choose to flow with God's plan. Be sensitive to the new things He is doing. Stay flexible to the Holy Spirit and know that ours is a God who directs, adjusts, moves, and corrects us. He is always working to bring us into perfection.

D~AY~ 21

"AN ARMY OF SHEEP LED BY A LION WOULD DEFEAT AN ARMY OF LIONS LED BY A SHEEP." — OLD ARAB PROVERB

What are the actions and attributes of a leader? What is it that makes him different from others?

1. A leader is always full of praise.

2. A leader learns to use the phrases "thank you" and "please" on his way to the top.

3. A leader is always growing.

4. A leader is possessed with his dreams.

5. A leader launches forth before success is certain.

6. A leader is not afraid of confrontation.

7. A leader talks about his own mistakes before talking about someone else's.

8. A leader is a person of honesty and integrity.

9. A leader has a good name.

10. A leader makes others better.

11. A leader is quick to praise and encourage the smallest amount of improvement.

12. A leader is genuinely interested in others.

13. A leader looks for opportunities to find someone doing something right.

14. A leader takes others up with him.

15. A leader responds to his own failures and acknowledges them before others have to discover and reveal them.

16. A leader never allows murmuring — from himself or others.

17. A leader is specific in what he expects.

18. A leaders holds accountable those who work with him.

19. A leader does what is right rather than what is popular.

20. A leader is a servant.

A leader is a lion, not a sheep.

DAY 22

PEOPLE ARE BORN ORIGINALS, BUT MOST DIE COPIES.

The call in your life is not a copy.

In this day of peer pressure, trends, and fads, we need to realize and accept that each person has been custom-made by God the Creator. Each of us has a unique and personal call upon our lives. We are to be our own selves and not copy other people.

Because I do a lot of work with churches, I come into contact with many different types of people. One time I talked over the phone with a pastor I had never met and who did not know me personally. We came to an agreement that I was to visit his church as a consultant. As we were closing our conversation and were setting a time to meet at the local airport, he asked me, "How will I know you when you get off the plane?"

"Oh, don't worry, pastor; I'll know you," I responded jokingly. "You all look alike."

271

The point of this humorous story is this: **be the person God has made YOU to be.**

The call of God upon our lives is the provision of God in our lives. We do not need to come up to the standards of anyone else. **The average person compares himself with others, but we Christians should always compare ourselves with the person God has called us to be.** That is our standard — God's unique plan and design for our lives. How the Lord chooses to deal with others has nothing to do with our individual call in life or God's timing and direction for us.

You and I can always find someone richer than we are, poorer than we are, or with more or less ability than we have. But how other people are, what they have, and what happens in their lives, has no effect upon our call. In Galatians 6:4 (TLB) we are admonished: *Let everyone be sure that he is doing his very best, for then he will have the personal satisfaction of work well done, and won't need to compare himself with someone else.*

God made you a certain way. You are unique. You are one of a kind. To copy others is to cheat yourself out of the fullness of what God has called you to be and to do.

So, choose to accept and become the person God has made you to be. Tap into the originality and creative genius of God in your life.

D~AY~ 23

STOP EVERY DAY AND
LOOK AT THE SIZE OF GOD.

Who is God? What is His personality like? What are His character traits?

According to the Bible, He is everlasting, just, caring, holy, divine, omniscient, omnipotent, omni-present and sovereign. He is light, perfection, abundance, salvation, wisdom, and love. He is the Creator, Savior, Deliverer, Redeemer, Provider, Healer, Advocate, and Friend. Never forget Who lives inside of you: *...the Lord...the great God, the great King above all gods* (Ps. 95:3 NIV).

John, the beloved disciple, tells us: *Ye are of God, little children, and have overcome them: because greater is he that is in you, than he that is in the world* (1 John 4:4). Period. Exclamation point. That settles it!

God and the devil are not equal, just opposite.

273

I travel by air quite often and one of the benefits is that every time I fly I get a glimpse of God's perspective. I like looking at my challenges from 37,000 feet in the air. **No problem is too large for God's intervention, and no person is too small for God's attention.**

God is always able. If you don't need miracles, you don't need God. Dave Bordon, a friend of mine, said it best: "I don't understand the situation, but I understand God."

The miraculous realm of God always has to do with multiplication, not addition.

God likens our life in Him to seedtime and harvest. Do you realize how miraculous that is? Let me give you a conservative example: Suppose one kernel of corn produces one stalk with two ears, each ear having 200 kernels. From those 400 kernels come 400 stalks with 160,000 kernels. All from one kernel planted only one season earlier.

Our confession to the Lord should be Jeremiah 32:17 (NIV): *"Ah, Sovereign Lord, you have made the heavens and the earth by your great power and outstretched arm. Nothing is too hard for you."*

God is bigger than _____ _____. Fill in the blank for your own life.

D<small>AY</small> 24

RETREAT TO ADVANCE.

Sometimes the most important and urgent thing we can do is get away to a peaceful and anointed spot.

This is one of the most powerful concepts that I personally have incorporated into my life. I'm sitting right now writing this book in a cabin up on a hill overlooking a beautiful lake, miles away from the nearest city.

As we choose to draw away for a time, we can see and hear much more clearly about how to go ahead. Jesus did this many times during His earthly life, especially just before and after major decisions. The Bible says, *...in quietness and in confidence shall be your strength...*(Is. 30:15). There's something invigorating and renewing about retreating to a quiet place of rest and peace. Silence is an environment in which great ideas are birthed.

There really are times when you should not see people, times when you should direct your whole attention toward God. I believe that every person should have a place of refuge, one out of the normal scope of living, one where he can "retreat to advance" and "focus in" with just the Lord and himself.

It is important to associate intently and as often as possible with your loftiest dreams. In Isaiah 40:31 we read, *But they that wait upon the Lord shall renew their strength; they shall mount up with wings as eagles; they shall run, and not be weary; and they shall walk, and not faint.* Learn to wait upon the Lord.

Make a regular appointment with yourself; it will be one of the most important you can ever have during the course of a week or a month. Choose to retreat to advance. See how much clearer you move forward with God as a result.

D~AY 25~

HAVE A READY WILL AND WALK,
NOT IDLE TIME AND TALK.

Acting on God's will is like riding a bicycle: if you don't go on, you go off!

Once we know God's will and timing, we should be instant to obey, taking action without delay. Delay and hesitation when God is telling us to do something now is sin. The longer we take to act on whatever God wants us to do, the more unclear His directives become. We need to make sure that we are on God's interstate highway and not in a cul-de-sac.

Ours is a God of velocity. He is a God of timing and direction. These two always go together. It is never wise to act upon only one or the other. Jumping at the first opportunity seldom leads to a happy landing. In Proverbs 25:8 the writer tells us, *Go not forth hastily to strive, lest thou know not what to do in the end thereof, when thy neighbour hath put thee to shame.* A famous saying holds that people can be divided into three groups: 1) those who make things happen,

277

2) those who watch things happen, and 3) those who wonder what's happening. Even the right direction taken at the wrong time is a bad decision.

Most people miss out on God's best in their lives because they're not prepared. The Bible warns us that we should be prepared continually. The Apostle Paul exhorts us: ...*be instant in season, out of season*... (2 Tim. 4:2).

There is a seasonality to God. In Ecclesiastes 3:1 we read: *To every thing there is a season, and a time to every purpose under the heaven.* Everything that you and I are involved in will have a spring (a time of planting and nurturing), a summer (a time of greatest growth), a fall (a time of harvest), and a winter (a time of decisions and planning).

Relax. Perceive, understand, and accept God's divine timing and direction.

DAY 26

WHEN WISDOM REIGNS,
IT POURS.

We should expect wisdom to be given to us.
The Bible says in James 1:5, *If any of you lack
wisdom, let him ask of God, that giveth to all men
liberally, and upbraideth not; and it shall be given him.*

**When you have heard God's voice, you have
heard His wisdom.** Thank God for His powerful
wisdom. It forces a passage through the strongest
barriers.

Wisdom is seeing everything from God's
perspective. It is knowing when and how to use
the knowledge that comes from the Lord. The old
saying is true, ''He who knows nothing, doubts
nothing.'' But it is also true that he who knows
has a solid basis for his belief.

Just think, we human beings have available
to us the wisdom of the Creator of the universe.
Yet **so few drink at the fountain of His wisdom;
most just rinse out their mouths.** Many may try

to live without the wisdom of the bread of life, but they will die in their efforts.

The world doesn't spend billions of dollars for wisdom. It spends billions in search of wisdom. Yet it is readily available to everyone who seeks its divine source.

There are ten steps to gaining godly wisdom:

1. Fear God (Ps. 111:10.)

2. Please God (Eccl. 2:26.)

3. Hear God (Prov. 2:6.)

4. Look to God (Prov. 3:13.)

5. Choose God's way (Prov. 8:10,11.)

6. Be humble before God (Prov. 11:2.)

7. Take God's advice (Prov. 13:10.)

8. Receive God's correction (Prov. 29:15.)

9. Pray to God (Eph. 1:17.)

10. Know the Son of God (1 Cor. 1:30.)

D<small>AY</small> 27

HEARING TELLS YOU THAT THE MUSIC IS PLAYING; LISTENING TELLS YOU WHAT THE SONG IS SAYING.

One of the least developed skills among us human beings is that of listening. There are really two different kinds of listening. There is the natural listening in interaction with other people, and there is spiritual listening to the voice of God.

It has been said, "Men are born with two ears, but only one tongue, which indicates that they were meant to listen twice as much as they talk." In natural communication, leaders always "monopolize the listening." **What we learn about another person will always result in a greater reward than what we tell him about ourselves.** We need to learn to listen and observe aggressively. We must try harder to truly listen, and not just to hear.

In regard to spiritual listening, Proverbs 8:34,35 (NIV) quotes wisdom who says:

281

Blessed is the man who listens to me, watching daily at my doors, waiting at my doorway.

For whoever finds me finds life and receives favor from the Lord.

There is great wisdom and favor to be gained by listening.

Proverbs 15:31 (NIV) says, *He who listens to a life-giving rebuke will be at home among the wise.* Listening allows us to maintain a teachable spirit. It increases our ''teach-ability.'' Those who give us a life-giving rebuke can be a great blessing to us.

The Bible teaches that we are to be quick to listen and slow to speak. (James 1:19.) We must never listen passively, especially to God. If we resist hearing, a hardening can take place in our lives. Callousness can develop. In Luke 16:31 (NIV), Jesus said of a certain group of people, ''. . . '*If they do not listen to Moses and the Prophets, they will not be convinced even if someone rises from the dead.*' '' The more we resist listening to the voice of God, the more hardened and less fine-tuned our hearing becomes.

There are results of spiritual hearing, as we see in Luke 8:15 (NIV). This passage relates to the parable of the sower: ''. . . *the seed on good soil stands for those with a noble and good heart, who hear the word, retain it, and by persevering produce a crop.''* Harvest is associated not only with persevering and good seed in good soil, but also with those people who hear the Word of God and retain it.

Fine-tune your natural and spiritual ears to listen and learn.

Dᴀʏ 28

GOD IS NOT YOUR PROBLEM;
GOD IS ON YOUR SIDE.

Some time ago I was eating at a Mexican fast food restaurant. As I stood in line for service I noticed in front of me a very poor elderly lady who looked like a street person. When it came her turn, she ordered some water and one taco. As I sat in the booth right next to her, I couldn't help but observe and be moved with compassion toward her. Shortly after I had begun my meal I went over to her and asked if I could buy some more food for her lunch. She looked at me and angrily asked, "Who are you?"

"Just a guy who wants to help you," I responded. She ignored me. I finished my meal about the same time she did, and we both got up to leave. I felt led to give her some money. In the parking lot I approached her and offered her some cash. Her only response to me was, "Stop bothering me." Then, she stormed off.

Immediately, the Lord showed me that this is often the way many of us respond to Him.

When He calls out to us, seeking to bless us, we act as though we don't even know Who He is. We respond to His offer of blessing by asking, "Who are You? What do You want from me?" The Lord, being the gracious God He is, continues to try to bless us. Yet we react by saying, "Stop bothering me." We walk off, just as this lady did, missing out on the rich blessings of the Lord.

It's not the absence of problems that gives us peace; it's God's presence with us in the problems. In Matthew 28:20, Jesus sent His disciples into all the world, ordering them to preach the Gospel to every creature: *Teaching them to observe all things whatsoever I have commanded you; and, lo, I am with you alway, even unto the end of the world.* In Romans 8:38,39 (NIV), the Apostle Paul writes, *For I am convinced that neither death nor life, neither angels nor demons, neither the present nor the future, nor any powers, neither height nor depth, nor anything else in all creation, will be able to separate us from the love of God that is in Christ Jesus our Lord.* In verse 31 he declares, *What, then, shall we say in response to this? If God is for us, who can be against us?* A paraphrase might be, "If God is for us, who cares who is against us?"

In Psalm 145:18 (NIV), we read, *The Lord is near to all who call on him, to all who call on him in truth.* James 4:8 (NIV) admonishes us, *Come near to God and he will come near to you.* In Acts 17:27

(NIV) Paul speaks: " 'For in him we live and move and have our being.' "

Thank God that we can, without hesitation and with full confidence, lean on His eternal faithfulness.

D<small>AY</small> 29

LEARN THE ALPHABET FOR SUCCESS.

A Action
B Belief
C Commitment
D Direction
E Enthusiasm
F Faith
G Goals
H Happiness
I Inspiration
J Judgment
K Knowledge
L Love
M Motivation
N Nonconformity
O Obedience
P Persistence
Q Quality
R Righteousness
S Steadfastness
T Thankfulness
U Uniqueness
V Vision

W Wisdom
X (E)xcellence
Y Yieldedness
Z Zeal

D AY 30

THE MEASURE OF A MAN IS NOT WHAT HE DOES ON SUNDAY, BUT RATHER WHO HE IS MONDAY THROUGH SATURDAY.

You don't have to come out of the Spirit realm. The same closeness, strength, joy, and direction you experience on Sunday, God intends for you to walk in the rest of the week. The devil is waiting to ambush you as you leave church. He wants to bring to your mind thoughts of fear, doubt, unbelief, and destruction.

That's why we believers must guard our minds and hearts. As spiritual creatures, we walk by faith, not by sight. (2 Cor. 5:7.) We are commanded to live in the Spirit and not in the natural.

A person whose eyes, ears, and mind are directed toward the world finds it difficult to hear God speaking to him. The Lord wants to talk to you at work, at lunch, at play — everywhere you go. Some of my greatest revelations from God have come not in my prayer closet, but rather "out of the blue" in the midst of my normal, everyday life.

Our inner man is always willing, but our natural man resists. That's what Jesus meant when He said to His disciples, *Watch and pray, that ye enter not into temptation; the spirit indeed is willing, but the flesh is weak* (Matt. 26:41).

The advantage of living and walking in the Spirit is that it keeps us on the right path. In Galatians 5:16,17 (NIV) the Apostle Paul writes: *So I say, live by the Spirit, and you will not gratify the desire of the sinful nature. For the sinful nature desires what is contrary to the Spirit, and the Spirit what is contrary to the sinful nature. They are in conflict with each other, so that you do not do what you want. But if you are led by the Spirit, you are not under law.*

Thank God that our relationship with Him is not a "some-time affair," it's an "all-the-time union." In the words of the old hymn, "He leadeth me! O blessed thought!"

DAY 31

GOD WILL USE YOU
RIGHT WHERE YOU ARE TODAY.

You don't need to do anything else for God to begin to use you now. You don't have to read another paperback book, listen to another cassette tape, memorize another scripture, plant another seed gift, or repeat another creed or confession. You don't even need to attend another church service before God will begin to make use of you.

God uses willing vessels, not brimming vessels. Throughout the Bible, in order to fulfill His plans for the earth, God used many people from all walks of life. He used:

1. Matthew, a government employee, who became an apostle.

2. Gideon, a common laborer, who became a valiant leader of men.

3. Jacob, a deceiver, whose name became Israel.

4. Deborah, a housewife, who became a judge.

5. Moses, a stutterer, who became a deliverer.

6. Jeremiah, a child, who fearlessly spoke the Word of the Lord.

7. Aaron, a servant, who became God's spokesman.

8. Nicodemus, a Pharisee, who became a defender of the faith.

9. David, a shepherd boy, who became a king.

10. Hosea, a marital failure, who prophesied to save Israel.

11. Joseph, a prisoner, who became prime minister.

12. Esther, an orphan, who became a queen.

13. Elijah, a homely man, who became a mighty prophet.

14. Joshua, an assistant, who became a conqueror.

15. James and John, fishermen, who became close disciples of Christ and were known as "sons of thunder."

16. Abraham, a nomad, who became the father of many nations.

17. Peter, a businessman, who became the rock on which Christ built His Church.

18. Jacob, a refugee, who became the father of the twelve tribes of Israel.

19. John the Baptist, a vagabond, who became the forerunner of Jesus.

20. Mary, an unknown virgin, who gave birth to the Son of God.

21. Nehemiah, a cupbearer, who built the wall of Jerusalem.

22. Shadrach, Meshach, and Abednego, Hebrew exiles, who became great leaders of the nation of Babylon.

23. Hezekiah, a son of an idolatrous father, who became a king renowned for doing right in the sight of the Lord.

24. Isaiah, a man of unclean lips, who prophesied the birth of God's Messiah.

25. Paul, a persecutor, who became the greatest missionary in history and author of two-thirds of the New Testament.

All God needs to use you is all of you!

A FINAL WORD

Be the whole person God called you to be. Don't settle for anything less. Don't look back. Look forward and decide today to take steps toward His plan for your life.

And remember First Thessalonians 5:24: *Faithful is he that calleth you, who also will do it.*

Endnote

[1]Adapted from *An Enemy Called Average* (Tulsa: Harrison House, 1990).

PART VI
READING THE BIBLE IN ONE YEAR:
A COMPLETE PROGRAM

January

1   Gen. 1-2; Ps. 1; Matt. 1-2
2   Gen. 3-4; Ps. 2; Matt. 3-4
3   Gen. 5-7; Ps. 3; Matt. 5
4   Gen. 8-9; Ps. 4; Matt. 6-7
5   Gen. 10-11; Ps. 5; Matt. 8-9
6   Gen. 12-13; Ps. 6; Matt. 10-11
7   Gen. 14-15; Ps. 7; Matt. 12
8   Gen. 16-17; Ps. 8; Matt. 13
9   Gen. 18-19; Ps. 9; Matt. 14-15
10 Gen. 20-21; Ps. 10; Matt. 16-17
11 Gen. 22-23; Ps. 11; Matt. 18
12 Gen. 24; Ps. 12; Matt. 19-20
13 Gen. 25-26; Ps. 13; Matt. 21
14 Gen. 27-28; Ps. 14; Matt. 22
15 Gen. 29-30; Ps. 15; Matt. 23
16 Gen. 31-32; Ps. 16; Matt. 24
17 Gen. 33-34; Ps. 17; Matt. 25
18 Gen. 35-36; Ps. 18; Matt. 26
19 Gen. 37-38; Ps. 19; Matt. 27
20 Gen. 39-40; Ps. 20; Matt. 28
21 Gen. 41-42; Ps. 21; Mark 1
22 Gen. 43-44; Ps. 22; Mark 2
23 Gen. 45-46; Ps. 23; Mark 3
24 Gen. 47-48; Ps. 24; Mark 4
25 Gen. 49-50; Ps. 25; Mark 5
26 Ex. 1-2; Ps. 26; Mark 6
27 Ex. 3-4; Ps. 27; Mark 7
28 Ex. 5-6; Ps. 28; Mark 8
29 Ex. 7-8; Ps. 29; Mark 9
30 Ex. 9-10; Ps. 30; Mark 10
31 Ex. 11-12; Ps. 31; Mark 11

February

1   Ex. 13-14; Ps. 32; Mark 12
2   Ex. 15-16; Ps. 33; Mark 13
3   Ex. 17-18; Ps. 34; Mark 14
4   Ex. 19-20; Ps. 35; Mark 15
5   Ex. 21-22; Ps. 36; Mark 16
6   Ex. 23-24; Ps. 37; Luke 1
7   Ex. 25-26; Ps. 38; Luke 2
8   Ex. 27-28; Ps. 39; Luke 3
9   Ex. 29-30; Ps. 40; Luke 4
10   Ex. 31-32; Ps. 41; Luke 5
11   Ex. 33-34; Ps. 42; Luke 6
12   Ex. 35-36; Ps. 43; Luke 7
13   Ex. 37-38; Ps. 44; Luke 8
14   Ex. 39-40; Ps. 45; Luke 9
15   Lev. 1-2; Ps. 46; Luke 10
16   Lev. 3-4; Ps. 47; Luke 11
17   Lev. 5-6; Ps. 48; Luke 12
18   Lev. 7-8; Ps. 49; Luke 13
19   Lev. 9-10; Ps. 50; Luke 14
20   Lev. 11-12; Ps. 51; Luke 15
21   Lev. 13; Ps. 52; Luke 16
22   Lev. 14; Ps. 53; Luke 17
23   Lev. 15-16; Ps. 54; Luke 18
24   Lev. 17-18; Ps. 55; Luke 19
25   Lev. 19-20; Ps. 56; Luke 20
26   Lev. 21-22; Ps. 57; Luke 21
27   Lev. 23-24; Ps. 58; Luke 22
28   Lev. 25
29   Ps. 59; Luke 23

March

1   Lev. 26-27; Ps. 60; Luke 24
2   Num. 1-2; Ps. 61; John 1
3   Num. 3-4; Ps. 62; John 2-3
4   Num. 5-6; Ps. 63; John 4
5   Num. 7; Ps. 64; John 5
6   Num. 8-9; Ps. 65; John 6
7   Num. 10-11; Ps. 66; John 7
8   Num. 12-13; Ps. 67; John 8
9   Num. 14-15; Ps. 68; John 9
10   Num. 16; Ps. 69; John 10
11   Num. 17-18; Ps. 70; John 11
12   Num. 19-20; Ps. 71; John 12
13   Num. 21-22; Ps. 72; John 13
14   Num. 23-24; Ps. 73; John 14-15
15   Num. 25-26; Ps. 74; John 16
16   Num. 27-28; Ps. 75; John 17
17   Num. 29-30; Ps. 76; John 18
18   Num. 31-32; Ps. 77; John 19
19   Num. 33-34; Ps. 78; John 20
20   Num. 35-36; Ps. 79; John 21
21   Deut. 1-2; Ps. 80; Acts 1
22   Deut. 3-4; Ps. 81; Acts 2
23   Deut. 5-6; Ps. 82; Acts 3-4
24   Deut. 7-8; Ps. 83; Acts 5-6
25   Deut. 9-10; Ps. 84; Acts 7
26   Deut. 11-12; Ps. 85; Acts 8
27   Deut. 13-14; Ps. 86; Acts 9
28   Deut. 15-16; Ps. 87; Acts 10
29   Deut. 17-18; Ps. 88; Acts 11-12
30   Deut. 19-20; Ps. 89; Acts 13
31   Deut. 21-22; Ps. 90; Acts 14

April

1   Deut. 23-24; Ps. 91; Acts 15
2   Deut. 25-27; Ps. 92; Acts 16
3   Deut. 28-29; Ps. 93; Acts 17
4   Deut. 30-31; Ps. 94; Acts 18
5   Deut. 32; Ps. 95; Acts 19
6   Deut. 33-34; Ps. 96; Acts 20
7   Josh. 1-2; Ps. 97; Acts 21
8   Josh. 3-4; Ps. 98; Acts 22
9   Josh. 5-6; Ps. 99; Acts 23
10 Josh. 7-8; Ps. 100; Acts 24-25
11 Josh. 9-10; Ps. 101; Acts 26
12 Josh. 11-12; Ps. 102; Acts 27
13 Josh. 13-14; Ps. 103; Acts 28
14 Josh. 15-16; Ps. 104; Rom. 1-2
15 Josh. 17-18; Ps. 105; Rom. 3-4
16 Josh. 19-20; Ps. 106; Rom. 5-6
17 Josh. 21-22; Ps. 107; Rom. 7-8
18 Josh. 23-24; Ps. 108; Rom. 9-10
19 Judg. 1-2; Ps. 109; Rom. 11-12
20 Judg. 3-4; Ps. 110; Rom. 13-14
21 Judg. 5-6; Ps. 111; Rom. 15-16
22 Judg. 7-8; Ps. 112; 1 Cor. 1-2
23 Judg. 9; Ps. 113; 1 Cor. 3-4
24 Judg. 10-11; Ps. 114; 1 Cor. 5-6
25 Judg. 12-13; Ps. 115; 1 Cor. 7
26 Judg. 14-15; Ps. 116; 1 Cor. 8-9
27 Judg. 16-17; Ps. 117; 1 Cor. 10
28 Judg. 18-19; Ps. 118; 1 Cor. 11
29 Judg. 20-21; Ps. 119:1-88; 1 Cor. 12
30 Ruth 1-4; Ps. 119:89-176; 1 Cor. 13

May

1   1 Sam. 1-2; Ps. 120; 1 Cor. 14
2   1 Sam. 3-4; Ps. 121; 1 Cor. 15
3   1 Sam. 5-6; Ps. 122; 1 Cor. 16
4   1 Sam. 7-8; Ps. 123; 2 Cor. 1
5   1 Sam. 9-10; Ps. 124; 2 Cor. 2-3
6   1 Sam. 11-12; Ps. 125; 2 Cor. 4-5
7   1 Sam. 13-14; Ps. 126; 2 Cor. 6-7
8   1 Sam. 15-16; Ps. 127; 2 Cor. 8
9   1 Sam. 17; Ps. 128; 2 Cor. 9-10
10 1 Sam. 18-19; Ps. 129; 2 Cor. 11
11 1 Sam. 20-21; Ps. 130; 2 Cor. 12
12 1 Sam. 22-23; Ps. 131; 2 Cor. 13
13 1 Sam. 24-25; Ps. 132; Gal. 1-2
14 1 Sam. 26-27; Ps. 133; Gal. 3-4
15 1 Sam. 28-29; Ps. 134; Gal. 5-6
16 1 Sam. 30-31; Ps. 135; Eph. 1-2
17 2 Sam. 1-2; Ps. 136; Eph. 3-4
18 2 Sam. 3-4; Ps. 137; Eph. 5-6
19 2 Sam. 5-6; Ps. 138; Phil. 1-2
20 2 Sam. 7-8; Ps. 139; Phil. 3-4
21 2 Sam. 9-10; Ps. 140; Col. 1-2
22 2 Sam. 11-12; Ps. 141; Col. 3-4
23 2 Sam. 13-14; Ps. 142; 1 Thess. 1-2
24 2 Sam. 15-16; Ps. 143; 1 Thess. 3-4
25 2 Sam. 17-18; Ps. 144; 1 Thess. 5
26 2 Sam. 19; Ps. 145; 2 Thess. 1-3
27 2 Sam. 20-21; Ps. 146; 1 Tim. 1-2
28 2 Sam. 22; Ps. 147; 1 Tim. 3-4
29 2 Sam. 23-24; Ps. 148; 1 Tim. 5-6
30 1 Kings 1; Ps. 149; 2 Tim. 1-2
31 1 Kings 2-3; Ps. 150; 2 Tim. 3-4

June

1   1 Kings 4-5; Prov. 1; Titus 1-3
2   1 Kings 6-7; Prov. 2; Philem.
3   1 Kings 8; Prov. 3; Heb. 1-2
4   1 Kings 9-10; Prov. 4; Heb. 3-4
5   1 Kings 11-12; Prov. 5; Heb. 5-6
6   1 Kings 13-14; Prov. 6; Heb. 7-8
7   1 Kings 15-16; Prov. 7; Heb. 9-10
8   1 Kings 17-18; Prov. 8; Heb. 11
9   1 Kings 19-20; Prov. 9; Heb. 12
10 1 Kings 21-22; Prov. 10; Heb. 13
11 2 Kings 1-2; Prov. 11; James 1
12 2 Kings 3-4; Prov. 12; James 2-3
13 2 Kings 5-6; Prov. 13; James 4-5
14 2 Kings 7-8; Prov. 14; 1 Pet. 1
15 2 Kings 9-10; Prov. 15; 1 Pet. 2-3
16 2 Kings 11-12; Prov. 16; 1 Pet. 4-5
17 2 Kings 13-14; Prov. 17; 2 Pet. 1-3
18 2 Kings 15-16; Prov. 18; 1 John 1-2
19 2 Kings 17; Prov. 19; 1 John 3-4
20 2 Kings 18-19; Prov. 20; 1 John 5
21 2 Kings 20-21; Prov. 21; 2 John
22 2 Kings 22-23; Prov. 22; 3 John
23 2 Kings 24-25; Prov. 23; Jude
24 1 Chron. 1; Prov. 24; Rev. 1-2
25 1 Chron. 2-3; Prov. 25; Rev. 3-5
26 1 Chron. 4-5; Prov. 26; Rev. 6-7
27 1 Chron. 6-7; Prov. 27; Rev. 8-10
28 1 Chron. 8-9; Prov. 28; Rev. 11-12
29 1 Chron. 10-11; Prov. 29; Rev. 13-14
30 1 Chron. 12-13; Prov. 30; Rev. 15-17

July

1	1 Chron. 14-15; Prov. 31; Rev. 18-19
2	1 Chron. 16-17; Ps. 1; Rev. 20-22
3	1 Chron. 18-19; Ps. 2; Matt. 1-2
4	1 Chron. 20-21; Ps. 3; Matt. 3-4
5	1 Chron. 22-23; Ps. 4; Matt. 5
6	1 Chron. 24-25; Ps. 5; Matt. 6-7
7	1 Chron. 26-27; Ps. 6; Matt. 8-9
8	1 Chron. 28-29; Ps. 7; Matt. 10-11
9	2 Chron. 1-2; Ps. 8; Matt. 12
10	2 Chron. 3-4; Ps. 9; Matt. 13
11	2 Chron. 5-6; Ps. 10; Matt. 14-15
12	2 Chron. 7-8; Ps. 11; Matt. 16-17
13	2 Chron. 9-10; Ps. 12; Matt. 18
14	2 Chron. 11-12; Ps. 13; Matt. 19-20
15	2 Chron. 13-14; Ps. 14; Matt. 21
16	2 Chron. 15-16; Ps. 15; Matt. 22
17	2 Chron. 17-18; Ps. 16; Matt. 23
18	2 Chron. 19-20; Ps. 17; Matt. 24
19	2 Chron. 21-22; Ps. 18; Matt. 25
20	2 Chron. 23-24; Ps. 19; Matt. 26
21	2 Chron. 25-26; Ps. 20; Matt. 27
22	2 Chron. 27-28; Ps. 21; Matt. 28
23	2 Chron. 29-30; Ps. 22; Mark 1
24	2 Chron. 31-32; Ps. 23; Mark 2
25	2 Chron. 33-34; Ps. 24; Mark 3
26	2 Chron. 35-36; Ps. 25; Mark 4
27	Ezra 1-2; Ps. 26; Mark 5
28	Ezra 3-4; Ps. 27; Mark 6
29	Ezra 5-6; Ps. 28; Mark 7
30	Ezra 7-8; Ps. 29; Mark 8
31	Ezra 9-10; Ps. 30; Mark 9

August

1   Neh. 1-2; Ps. 31; Mark 10
2   Neh. 3-4; Ps. 32; Mark 11
3   Neh. 5-6; Ps. 33; Mark 12
4   Neh. 7, Ps. 34; Mark 13
5   Neh. 8-9; Ps. 35; Mark 14
6   Neh. 10-11; Ps. 36; Mark 15
7   Neh. 12-13; Ps. 37; Mark 16
8   Esth. 1-2; Ps. 38; Luke 1
9   Esth. 3-4; Ps. 39; Luke 2
10   Esth. 5-6; Ps. 40; Luke 3
11   Esth. 7-8; Ps. 41; Luke 4
12   Esth. 9-10; Ps. 42; Luke 5
13   Job 1-2; Ps. 43; Luke 6
14   Job 3-4; Ps. 44; Luke 7
15   Job 5-6; Ps. 45; Luke 8
16   Job 7-8; Ps. 46; Luke 9
17   Job 9-10; Ps. 47; Luke 10
18   Job 11-12; Ps. 48; Luke 11
19   Job 13-14; Ps. 49; Luke 12
20   Job 15-16; Ps. 50; Luke 13
21   Job 17-18; Ps. 51; Luke 14
22   Job 19-20; Ps. 52; Luke 15
23   Job 21-22; Ps. 53; Luke 16
24   Job 23-25; Ps. 54; Luke 17
25   Job 26-28; Ps. 55; Luke 18
26   Job 29-30; Ps. 56; Luke 19
27   Job 31-32; Ps. 57; Luke 20
28   Job 33-34; Ps. 58; Luke 21
29   Job 35-36; Ps. 59; Luke 22
30   Job 37-38; Ps. 60; Luke 23
31   Job 39-40; Ps. 61; Luke 24

September

1   Job 41-42; Ps. 62; John 1
2   Eccl. 1-2; Ps. 63; John 2-3
3   Eccl. 3-4; Ps. 64; John 4
4   Eccl. 5-6; Ps. 65; John 5
5   Eccl. 7-8; Ps. 66; John 6
6   Eccl. 9-10; Ps. 67; John 7
7   Eccl. 11-12; Ps. 68; John 8
8   Song of Sol. 1-2; Ps. 69; John 9
9   Song of Sol. 3-4; Ps. 70; John 10
10 Song of Sol. 5-6; Ps. 71; John 11
11 Song of Sol. 7-8; Ps. 72; John 12
12 Isaiah 1-2; Ps. 73; John 13
13 Isaiah 3-5; Ps. 74; John 14-15
14 Isaiah 6-8; Ps. 75; John 16
15 Isaiah 9-10; Ps. 76; John 17
16 Isaiah 11-13; Ps. 77; John 18
17 Isaiah 14-15; Ps. 78; John 19
18 Isaiah 16-17; Ps. 79; John 20
19 Isaiah 18-19; Ps. 80; John 21
20 Isaiah 20-22; Ps. 81; Acts 1
21 Isaiah 23-24; Ps. 82; Acts 2
22 Isaiah 25-26; Ps. 83; Acts 3-4
23 Isaiah 27-28; Ps. 84; Acts 5-6
24 Isaiah 29-30; Ps. 85; Acts 7
25 Isaiah 31-32; Ps. 86; Acts 8
26 Isaiah 33-34; Ps. 87; Acts 9
27 Isaiah 35-36; Ps. 88; Acts 10
28 Isaiah 37-38; Ps. 89; Acts 11-12
29 Isaiah 39-40; Ps. 90; Acts 13
30 Isaiah 41-42; Ps. 91; Acts 14

October

1   Isaiah 43-44; Ps. 92; Acts 15
2   Isaiah 45-46; Ps. 93; Acts 16
3   Isaiah 47-48; Ps. 94; Acts 17
4   Isaiah 49-50; Ps. 95; Acts 18
5   Isaiah 51-52; Ps. 96; Acts 19
6   Isaiah 53-54; Ps. 97; Acts 20
7   Isaiah 55-56; Ps. 98; Acts 21
8   Isaiah 57-58; Ps. 99; Acts 22
9   Isaiah 59-60; Ps. 100; Acts 23
10 Isaiah 61-62; Ps. 101; Acts 24-25
11 Isaiah 63-64; Ps. 102; Acts 26
12 Isaiah 65-66; Ps. 103; Acts 27
13 Jer. 1-2; Ps. 104; Acts 28
14 Jer. 3-4; Ps. 105; Rom. 1-2
15 Jer. 5-6; Ps. 106; Rom. 3-4
16 Jer. 7-8; Ps. 107; Rom. 5-6
17 Jer. 9-10; Ps. 108; Rom. 7-8
18 Jer. 11-12; Ps. 109; Rom. 9-10
19 Jer. 13-14; Ps. 110; Rom. 11-12
20 Jer. 15-16; Ps. 111; Rom. 13-14
21 Jer. 17-18; Ps. 112; Rom. 15-16
22 Jer. 19-20; Ps. 113; 1 Cor. 1-2
23 Jer. 21-22; Ps. 114; 1 Cor. 3-4
24 Jer. 23-24; Ps. 115; 1 Cor. 5-6
25 Jer. 25-26; Ps. 116; 1 Cor. 7
26 Jer. 27-28; Ps. 117; 1 Cor. 8-9
27 Jer. 29-30; Ps. 118; 1 Cor. 10
28 Jer. 31-32; Ps. 119:1-64; 1 Cor. 11
29 Jer. 33-34; Ps. 119:65-120; 1 Cor. 12
30 Jer. 35-36; Ps. 119:121-176; 1 Cor. 13
31 Jer. 37-38; Ps. 120; 1 Cor. 14

November

1	Jer. 39-40; Ps. 121; 1 Cor. 15
2	Jer. 41-42; Ps. 122; 1 Cor. 16
3	Jer. 43-44; Ps. 123; 2 Cor. 1
4	Jer. 45-46; Ps. 124; 2 Cor. 2-3
5	Jer. 47-48; Ps. 125; 2 Cor. 4-5
6	Jer. 49-50; Ps. 126; 2 Cor. 6-7
7	Jer. 51-52; Ps. 127; 2 Cor. 8
8	Lam. 1-2; Ps. 128; 2 Cor. 9-10
9	Lam. 3; Ps. 129; 2 Cor. 11
10	Lam. 4-5; Ps. 130; 2 Cor. 12
11	Ezek. 1-2; Ps. 131; 2 Cor. 13
12	Ezek. 3-4; Ps. 132; Gal. 1-2
13	Ezek. 5-6; Ps. 133; Gal. 3-4
14	Ezek. 7-8; Ps. 134; Gal. 5-6
15	Ezek. 9-10; Ps. 135; Eph. 1-2
16	Ezek. 11-12; Ps. 136; Eph. 3-4
17	Ezek. 13-14; Ps. 137; Eph. 5-6
18	Ezek. 15-16; Ps. 138; Phil. 1-2
19	Ezek. 17-18; Ps. 139; Phil. 3-4
20	Ezek. 19-20; Ps. 140; Col. 1-2
21	Ezek. 21-22; Ps. 141; Col. 3-4
22	Ezek. 23-24; Ps. 142; 1 Thess. 1-2
23	Ezek. 25-26; Ps. 143; 1 Thess. 3-4
24	Ezek. 27-28; Ps. 144; 1 Thess. 5
25	Ezek. 29-30; Ps. 145; 2 Thess. 1-3
26	Ezek. 31-32; Ps. 146; 1 Tim. 1-2
27	Ezek. 33-34; Ps. 147; 1 Tim. 3-4
28	Ezek. 35-36; Ps. 148; 1 Tim. 5-6
29	Ezek. 37-38; Ps. 149; 2 Tim. 1-2
30	Ezek. 39-40; Ps. 150; 2 Tim. 3-4

December

1	Ezek. 41-42; Prov. 1; Titus 1-3
2	Ezek. 43-44; Prov. 2; Philem.
3	Ezek. 45-46; Prov. 3; Heb. 1-2
4	Ezek. 47-48; Prov. 4; Heb. 3-4
5	Dan. 1-2; Prov. 5; Heb. 5-6
6	Dan. 3-4; Prov. 6; Heb. 7-8
7	Dan. 5-6; Prov. 7; Heb. 9-10
8	Dan. 7-8; Prov. 8; Heb. 11
9	Dan. 9-10; Prov. 9; Heb. 12
10	Dan. 11-12; Prov. 10; Heb. 13
11	Hos. 1-3; Prov. 11; James 1-3
12	Hos. 4-6; Prov. 12; James 4-5
13	Hos. 7-8; Prov. 13; 1 Pet. 1
14	Hos. 9-11; Prov. 14; 1 Pet. 2-3
15	Hos. 12-14; Prov. 15; 1 Pet. 4-5
16	Joel 1-3; Prov. 16; 2 Pet. 1-3
17	Amos 1-3; Prov. 17; 1 John 1-2
18	Amos 4-6; Prov. 18; 1 John 3-4
19	Amos 7-9; Prov. 19; 1 John 5
20	Obad.; Prov. 20; 2 John
21	Jonah 1-4; Prov. 21; 3 John
22	Mic. 1-4; Prov. 22; Jude
23	Mic. 5-7; Prov. 23; Rev. 1-2
24	Nah. 1-3; Prov. 24; Rev. 3-5
25	Hab. 1-3; Prov. 25; Rev. 6-7
26	Zeph. 1-3; Prov. 26; Rev. 8-10
27	Hag. 1-2; Prov. 27; Rev. 11-12
28	Zech. 1-4; Prov. 28; Rev. 13-14
29	Zech. 5-9; Prov. 29; Rev. 15-17
30	Zech. 10-14; Prov. 30; Rev. 18-19
31	Mal. 1-4; Prov. 31; Rev. 20-22

Recommended Reading

1. *The Bible*
2. *You and Your Network* — Fred Smith
3. *How To Win Friends and Influence People* — Dale Carnegie
4. *See You at the Top* — Zig Ziglar
5. *Stay in the Game* — Van Crouch
6. *An Enemy Called Average* — John Mason
7. *University of Success* — Og Mandino
8. *Working Smart* — Michael LeBoeuf
9. *Maximized Manhood* — Ed Cole
10. *Rhythm of Life* — Richard Exley

Additional copies of

Dare To Succeed

are available from your local bookstore

or from:

P. O. Box 55388
Tulsa, Oklahoma 74155